END-TIME PROPHECY
Part

C000101683

The Prophetic Framework

by Derek Walker

END-TIME PROPHECY

Contents

Introduction   2

Part 1 - The Prophetic Framework   5
   Key 1: Interpret prophecy literally   8
   Key 2: Dispensationalism   13
   Key 3: Premillennialism   19
   Key 4: Israel and the Church   30
   Key 5: The Sufferings and the Glory   36
   Key 6: The Kingdom Offered   42
   Key 7: The Kingdom Rejected and Postponed   45
   Key 8: The Mystery of the Church   85
   Key 9: Prophetic Gaps   88
   Key 10: The Tribulation   97
   Key 11: The Framework Prophecies   99
      1- Daniel's 70 Weeks   99
      2- The Olivet Discourse   112
      3- The Revelation to John   149
   Key 12: Futurism   150

Appendix: Daniel's 70 Weeks   153
Appendix: A Harmony of the Olivet Discourse   174

Part 2 - The Church in Prophecy (see Book 2)

Part 3 - The Tribulation (see Book 3)

Part 4 - The Eternal Reign of Christ (see Book 4)

INTRODUCTION

This Series of 4 Books aims to provide a systematic introduction to Bible Prophecy, describing future events in their chronological order, and showing how God is working out His Purposes and fulfilling His Promises and Covenants.

"Worship God! For the testimony of Jesus is the spirit of prophecy." (Revelation 19:10).   It is my prayer that as you study Bible Prophecy, you will receive an exciting revelation of the glory of the Lord Jesus Christ.   Bible-Prophecy gives us a firm assurance and a certain hope that God is sovereignly establishing His Kingdom.   Whereas knowing the prophecies that have already been fulfilled authenticates scripture and builds our faith; knowing prophecy that is as yet unfulfilled builds our hope, giving us an anchor for our soul, that holds us steady for life in our troubled times.   **"Therefore, since we are receiving a Kingdom which cannot be shaken, let us have grace, by which we may serve God acceptably with reverence and godly fear"** (Hebrews 12:28).

Bible Prophecy is important. If it were not so, God would not have devoted one third of His Bible to prophecy!   It must be important to God as shown by the large amount of scripture given to it. God has much to tells us about the future, for He wants us to understand His plans and purposes, so that we can guide our lives by them. If we ignore it or dismiss it as unimportant then we are dismissing a large portion of God's Word. If we do not understand Bible Prophecy we are ignorant of a third of the Bible. As a result we will be the losers, for all scripture is given for our benefit, to enable us to live in God's plans and purposes.

The study of Bible Prophecy has many purposes:

It glorifies God, revealing His wisdom, power and sovereignty in fulfilling His purposes.   He is the Alpha and Omega. He knows the end from the beginning.

Bible Prophecy glorifies the Lord Jesus Christ as it reveals His past work of salvation and His future dominion. Prophecy is Christ-centred for it is all about Him: **"the testimony of Jesus is the spirit of prophecy"** (Revelation 19:10). Therefore it exalts Christ and keeps Him in the centre of our vision.

Prophecy gives us comfort and hope for the future, especially for believers suffering hard times. The 3 things that are of eternal value that we gain through God's Word are FAITH, HOPE and LOVE. It is through the study of the prophetic scriptures that HOPE is imparted to our hearts and minds. If we do not know Bible Prophecy, we are spiritually lacking in one of the big three areas of life. It puts the helmet of the HOPE of salvation firmly on our heads, covering our minds and protecting our thoughts, so that we can see through the present problems of this evil age to the victorious conclusion, for it reminds us that God is ultimately in control and working His purposes out. Therefore it stabilises and encourages us as we live through dangerous times. Knowing our future and the future of the world gives us wisdom, peace and focus for living our lives now in God's plan and purpose. Without a knowledge of Bible Prophecy our hearts and minds do not have the protection that God wants us to have and that He has provided for us in His Word. As we study Bible-Prophecy we are putting on our Helmet of Hope (confident expectancy of future Salvation) over our minds.

Knowing Bible Prophecy is good for our mental health, for it gives us the big picture, the panaoramic view of God's Purposes. We can get so caught up in our own small world, and as a result lose the big picture along with the inspiration, focus and balance it provides. It is healthy to see our problems in perspective and that is what Bible Prophecy provides. God is magnified and our problems don't seem so great, when we see the grand scheme of things. If God is sovereignly bringing His purposes to pass and will usher in an eternal age of glory, then surely He is able to work all things in our life for our good.

Prophecy provides strong warnings for those who persist in unbelief. It therefore stimulates us to serve the Lord and witness to Him, knowing that He is coming soon to judge the lost, and then it will be too late for them to repent.

Bible Prophecy alerts us and gets up ready for the Coming of the Lord. It makes us conscious that He is coming soon to judge and reward believers for our faithfulness in serving Him. This was a major motivation for the first believers to live lives of holiness and fruitful service and so it is for us who live in the last days of the Church Age. It will cause us to live each day in the light and excitement of His imminant Appearing, knowing that anytime soon we will stand before Him and give an account. So many believers are asleep and unprepared. To a large extent this is because they are ignorant of the prophetic scriptures.

This Book also demonstrates that we are now living in the Close of this Age, in the last generation before Christ's Return!

This series of 4 Books form a comprehensive guide to End-Time Prophecy that will serve as a useful reference, as world-events continue to unfold before our eyes as the world moves towards the climax revealed in the Bible. Therefore it is hoped that the reader will gain understanding of the times he lives in and motivation to live his life pleasing to God and to make it count for the Lord

Just as in building a House, in order to understand Bible-Prophecy, we must first lay the Foundation and put up the basic overall Framework, and then fill in the rest. After establishing the Framework in this Book (Part One of the Series), we will then fill in the substance of the House, using the abundant prophetic material provided in the Bible. I leave it to the reader's judgement, how well these pieces have been fitted together into their correct place.

Therefore, this Book (Part One) gives the foundational principles (keys) for understanding the prophetic scriptures, and establishes the overall Framework of Bible Prophecy. These principles are essential to understanding the rest.

Part Two (Book 2) covers the Church Age and the Rapture.

Part Three (Book 3) covers the events of the Tribulation (which comes after the Church Age) as described particularly in the Book of Revelation.

Part Four (Book 4) describes the Battle of Armageddon and the Second Coming of Jesus Christ to judge and rule the world. Then it brings the story to its glorious conclusion with Christ's Millennial Reign and the Eternal State.

Part 1 - The Prophetic Framework

We all desire to know the future, for it would give us a great guide to our life now. This is not just our idle curiosity, for such knowledge would be a great advantage for our plans and preparations and in giving direction to our lives.

Can we know the future?

Yes - through a study of Bible Prophecy!

The Importance of Prophecy. Through prophecy God declares the end from the beginning proving that He is the unique Sovereign God of eternity:

**"I am God, and there is no other; I am God, and there is none like Me, declaring the end from the beginning,
and from ancient times things that are not yet done, saying,
`My counsel shall stand, and I will do all My pleasure"** (Isaiah 46:9,10).

Thus first of all Prophecy glorifies God.

Moreover, if we judge the importance of a subject by the amount of coverage it is given in the Bible, then we would have to admit that Prophecy is one of the most important areas of study for a Christian, one that will greatly impact and improve his life.   Yet, the Church today generally has a different opinion, relegating the study of prophecy to an optional extra, a side-issue, and as a result many neglect vast portions of the Word of God.   The Book of Revelation, a book composed almost entirely of prophecy, is uniquely stamped by God as having great importance. Unlike any of the other books it starts with a pronouncement of blessing upon all those who read and accept it:

"Blessed is he who reads and those who hear the words of this prophecy, and keep those things which are written in it; for the time is near" (Revelation 1:3).

Moreover, it is the only book that ends with a curse on those who do not accept it in its entirety: **"I testify to everyone who hears the words of the prophecy** of this book: **If anyone adds to these things, God will add to him the plagues that are written in this book; and if anyone takes away from the words of the book of this prophecy, God shall take away his part from the Book of Life, from the holy city, and from the things which are written in this book"** (Revelation 22:18,19).   If anyone should doubt the importance that God gives to Prophecy, those doubts should now be settled!   In particular, this is a command to interpret the Book literally (see Key 1, page 8 on), so that we accept it fully as written and don't make it what we want it to mean.   We are warned against changing the meaning of the Book, just because we don't like it. We are not to add or take away from the plain meaning of this Book of Prophecy. Yet this is exactly what people do, who do not interpret Prophecy literally.   Thus the only safe method of prophetic interpretation is to take its plain (literal) sense.

Christians need to know what the Bible says about the future ('Eschatology') **for it affects how we live today and the causes we give ourselves to.**   It helps us flow with God's purposes for this time and not to be overly disturbed by events because we know where history is going.

But where do we start?

The Jigsaw Puzzle of Prophecy.   The Bible contains a massive amount of prophetic material, given by God to many different prophets over thousands of years, yet all combining to produce a unified vision of the future.
However, each prophecy is just a glimpse of the bigger picture.
It is like one piece of a 5000-piece jigsaw puzzle.   The Bible contains all the pieces, but they are not all neatly arranged in order in one book, but scattered all over the Bible, and so it is up to us to study and put these pieces together in the right way, so that we can see the whole picture.

TO SEE THE TRUE PROPHETIC PANORAMA, we must put together the many pieces of the jigsaw of prophetic scriptures into their right place.

When doing a big jigsaw, one helpful step is to gather together pieces that look similar, because they are likely to be close together in the picture.

Likewise, we shall see that the prophets looked into the future and saw events in certain different and distinguishable time-periods (such as the First-Coming of Christ, the Church-Age, the Rapture, the Tribulation, The Second-Coming of Christ, the Millennium, and the Eternal-State). By learning the characteristics of each of these times, we will be able to discern roughly where each piece fits.

It is easy to go wrong and put the pieces together incorrectly which leads to a distorted picture. You can't put the pieces together any old way. You know when you have got it right - all the pieces fit with one another perfectly. If you have an interpretation, it must harmonise with the rest of prophetic scripture. If you think you have found a contradiction, it is simply that you are not fitting the pieces together correctly, for God does not contradict Himself:

Another vital principle in doing a big jigsaw, is to do the outer frame first. You don't just jump into the middle and get started. Likewise with Prophecy, we need to proceed carefully and construct the FRAME first (the overall scheme or Framework). Then we will be able to see more clearly how to fit the other pieces in, and thus fill in all the details. Thus to understand prophecy rightly, we must first grasp the foundational principles (Keys). If we don't do this first, but just look at prophetic scriptures randomly, then we won't fit the pieces together correctly and we will get a distorted and incomplete picture.

The aim of this Book (Part 1) is to build this Framework.

Thus, we now present the 12 main Keys for understanding Prophecy.
Once we grasp the fundamental principles then we will see how wonderfully and neatly all the pieces fit together and the various issues and questions like, 'Will the Church go through the Tribulation?' will be easily answered.

KEY 1: Interpret Prophecy Literally.

This is the **first key** to understanding all scripture. The fundamental issue to settle is the correct rules of interpreting Bible Prophecy. Different prophetic viewpoints mostly come from differing approaches to interpretation. Literal or Plain Interpretation means we must interpret prophecy like all other scripture - in its plain meaning according to the laws of language, as the author intended it and as the original hearers would have understood it. This has far-reaching consequences. Literal interpretation requires us to read any passage in context, so that our understanding of it must fit with what comes before and after it. Moreover since we believe the whole Bible together forms the complete Word of God, our interpretation must also fit (agree) with the rest of Scripture.

Opposing the **LITERAL** approach is an **ALLEGORICAL** (spiritualising) approach to prophecy, which allows people to change (twist) the obvious meaning of a verse, to fit their preconceived ideas. The literal approach is to take all scripture in its plain meaning, unless it does not make sense and is obviously meant to be interpreted symbolically. However, the other approach often rejects the literal meaning of a scripture and tries to replace it by a 'spiritual' interpretation, even when its plain meaning makes perfect sense. Literal interpretation does not mean we cannot see spiritual parallels to the literal fulfilment or make spiritual applications of it, but first of all, it upholds the literal fulfilment of the prophecy.

Now prophetic literature (like the Book of Revelation) contains much language that is obviously symbolic and pictorial, to help us understand and visualise unfamiliar spiritual realities by comparing them to familiar things around us. Literal interpretation means we interpret obvious symbolic language accordingly.

Some examples of symbolic language are:
1. Obvious FIGURES OF SPEECH (e.g 'thorn in the flesh' - 2Corinthians 12:7)
2. PARABLES. In this Series of Books on Prophecy, we interpret many parables allegorically, for they are obviously symbolic stories to teach spiritual truth. Although parables make perfect literal sense (and so should be understood first on that level, they are obviously given to communicate a parallel spiritual truth.

3. VISIONARY PICTURES often include many symbols (see Revelation 12).

4. As well as these examples, there is also sometimes a TYPOLOGICAL (symbolic) APPLICATION of a scripture which makes perfect literal sense. God ordains certain events of scripture to reveal in picture form some greater reality that has yet to happen (for example, Abraham offering up Isaac as a sacrifice, is a type or picture of the Father offering up the Son on the Cross). **When we make a typological application, we are not denying the literal meaning of the Scripture.** Thus for example in Part 2, we will make the case that the 7 literal Churches of Revelation 2,3 are prophetic types of the 7 phases of Church history. Also, in Part 3, we will argue that 7 Times (of 2520 days) is a type of 7 Times (of 2520 years) of Gentile Dominion. But in each of these cases we uphold the literal fulfilment of the original event.

Now when the Bible uses symbolic (coded) language, this does not mean that the meaning is obscure and mysterious. Many don't read Revelation because they think it is impossible to understand. But the very meaning of 'revelation' is an unveiling of that which was hidden. It is given in order to be understood. Scripture becomes clear as we come to it humbly, reading it according to the principle of literal interpretation, and asking the help of the Holy-Spirit.

When the Bible is clearly using symbols, that does not mean we are free to interpret them any way we would like. The Bible will always supplies the correct interpretation of each symbol, so it tells you how you can crack the code!

First of all look in the immediate context.
For example after seeing a vision John was told:

"The mystery of the 7 stars which you saw in My right hand, and the 7 golden lampstands: the 7 stars are the angels of the 7 churches, and the 7 lampstands which you saw are the 7 churches" (Revelation 1:20).

Sometimes you have to look elsewhere in the Bible for the meaning of a symbol. Thus Paul's 'thorn in the flesh' (2Cor 12:7) was not a literal thorn or he would have pulled it out. Neither does it symbolise a sickness as many believe.

If we look for a parallel use of this idiom elsewhere in scripure we will find that it represents trouble, persecution and opposition from people (Numbers 33:55). Likewise we would say today that they were 'a pain in the neck'. Paul was praying for God to deliver him from those who were opposing and persecuting him (especially the religious Jews). Since the whole Bible is the Word of God, it always uses symbols consistently.

Thus literal interpretation simply means that you read the Bible in its PLAIN MEANING, as the writer intended. For example, when a prophet made a promise to Israel, he meant 'Israel' not 'the Church' (he didn't even know about the Church!). A major error made by those who don't read prophecy literally is to replace 'Israel' by 'the Church.' Prophecies to Israel are not to be changed into prophecies of the Church. However we can sometimes apply God's promises to Israel to the Church, as long as in doing this we don't deny their plain meaning and application to Israel (the link is the New-Covenant). 'Spiritualisers' of scripture come along with a mind set and change the original meaning to fit it into their viewpoint. Clearly this is an unsafe way to read scripture. So taking a literal approach limits us to taking scripture in its straightforward meaning and obvious symbolism is interpreted as such.

Three examples to test if you read prophecy literally:
(1) Isaiah 11:6-9: **'the wolf will lie down with the lamb'.** The transformation of the animal kingdom or harmony of all kinds of people in the Church?

(2) Revelation 7:1-8: Will there literally be 144,000 evangelists from Israel, 12,000 from each tribe, or is this a symbolic of the Church?

(3) Revelation 20:1-7 Will there be a literal 1,000 years as described here, or is it simply symbolic of a long time-period?

We can still bring forth spiritual types, analogies and allegories from a literal understanding as long as we don't deny their primary and plain meaning. In fact, it is essential to grasp their plain meaning before making spiritual

application from them.   Moreover we can apply to the Church, God's promises
to Israel concerning the New Covenant (see Jeremiah 31:31-34 and
Hebrews 8:7-13), because although the New Covenant belongs first of
all to Israel, we have been baptised into Christ (Abraham's seed), and thus
we qualify to participate fully in the spiritual blessings of the New Covenant.

The main reason that there are so many views and interpretations on Bible
prophecy causing much confusion, is the failure to take the Bible literally in this
area. (While there are, of course, differences among those who take it literally,
these are relatively minor).   The ultimate root of this failure to believe the
prophetic scriptures according to their plain meaning is of course unbelief.

We are further encouraged to interpret Prophecy plainly because:

1. Bible Believers use literal interpretation to interpret all other areas of scripture
doctrine. But many spiritualise prophecy. Why should prophecy be the
exception?   This leads to inconsistencies. For example some prophecies to
Israel (the negative ones) are taken literally, while the positive ones are
spiritualised and applied to the Church.

2. Without literal interpretation, there is no way to know the real meaning
and no control over how to interpret scripture.   It leaves the door open for wild
uncontrolled interpretation. It means that we are free to supply whatever
meaning we want. Literal interpretation is the only way to be in submission
to God's Word (spiritualising allows us to make it mean whatever we want).
Otherwise we are in danger of tampering with the word of God which can have
serious consequences as Revelation 22:18,19 warns us strongly. We are not
to add to it meanings that are not there, or take away from what it is saying,
but simply to discover what it is saying in plain language and submit to it.

3.   Some 20% of Bible prophecy has already been fulfilled.
HOW? Literally (e.g Jesus was born in literal Bethlehem - Micah 5:2).
Will not the rest be fulfilled likewise?

4. If prophecy is not fulfilled literally how will you know if it has been fulfilled or not? If someone predicts you will get a job in Nottingham next month but you instead you get a job in Oxford, is the prophecy fulfilled?   What would you say to someone who says 'it is fulfilled, for Oxford is spiritual Nottingham'? Or what if a prophecy said you would get a million pounds tomorrow, but nothing arrived and then you were told the prophecy really meant that you would just feel like a million pounds!   Would you consider it fulfilled?

5. If prophecy to Israel is not fulfilled literally to Israel, then God is a deceiver. What if God has made promises to you, only to be told later: 'I did not mean you, Tom, I was giving the promise to someone else - 'spiritual Tom'! If God is not faithful to His promises to Israel but breaks His Word to them, then we could have no assurance that He will be faithful to His promises to us!

6. The reward of reading prophecy literally means the Bible comes alive. It makes sense and it all fits together as a masterpiece, as I hope to show. Much truth is lost in denying the obvious meaning.   In previous times it was harder to believe that prophecy would be fulfilled literally. The idea of Israel coming back to the land and of various events of the Book of Revelation taking place may have seemed impossible.   But today, as we see the world change scientifically and politically it seems to be right up to date.   Now, Bible- believers have no excuse not to believe that it will all be literally fulfilled.

7. Jesus understood and interpreted prophecy literally (compare Daniel 9:27 and Matthew 24:15).   Moreover, as we have already pointed out, His final words of warning (Rev 22:18-20) require us to interpret prophecy in its plain meaning.

8.   The national rebirth of the nation of Israel in 1948, against all odds, in fulfilment of Bible Prophecy, is a sure proof that God is fulfilling prophecy literally. When certain courageous believers in the 19th Century pointed out that Israel must be restored to her land they they laughed at by those who did not take prophecy literally, because it seemed so impossible.   How could a nation be reborn after 2000 years? Such a thing had never been heard of. Yet through the fires of the Holocaust Israel came to birth just as the Bible said it would, and it took its place as the major sign that we are now in the end-times.

Key 2: Dispensationalism.

I believe that taking a **literal interpretation** of the prophetic scriptures
leads to **Dispensationalism, Pre-Millennialism, and Futurism.**
We will explain these terms in due course.

Dispensationalism is based on a literal interpretation of scripture. The word
sometimes translated 'dispensation' is used for the management, administration
or stewardship of a household. Dispensationalism, in its basic form, describes
how God manages and rules the world. All time is divided into dispensations
(extended periods under a definite kind of administration of God). When God
intervenes to change the way He runs His household, there is a dispensational
change. Many things remain the same, but whatever is to change is explained
by God at the time. This pattern is reflected in the phrase **'the times** (chronos)
and seasons (kairos)' of God, which we are expected to understand
(1Thessalonians 5:1). **'Chronos'** is an extended period of time; whereas
'kairos' usually describes a special moment in time, or a short transitional time,
when a major change is effected, bringing about a new 'chronos'. This has
application to our own lives, but as far as history and prophecy is concerned,
each major Divine 'kairos' intervention (either of judgement or of grace) moves
God's dealings with man into a new phase, bringing in a new dispensation.
Thus, understanding the dispensations helps us to keep track of God's
progressive revelation through time.

God began by dealing with mankind as a whole (the Age of the Gentiles),
then after 2,000 years He started through Abraham to form a special, separated
Nation (the Age of Israel), and then after another 2000 years, He formed a new
body of people called out of both Israel and the nations (the Age of the Church).
Then after 6000 years Christ will be personally present on earth ruling as King
over all 3 groups for 1000 years (the Age of Christ), thus completing the Divine
Week of 7 DAYS or 7000 years of time. Finally, at the end of time all the
redeemed will be united into one People of God for all Eternity (Ephesians 1:10).
See also pages 146-148 for more on God's overall structure of Time.

Thus in the outworking of God's Plan of Redemption and in His management of mankind, there are 3 distinct groups that God deals with: **"the Gentiles, Israel and the Church"** (1Corinthians 10:32).

The focus of God's Plan of Redemption often changes from group to group as the dispensations change. God has a distinct plan, purpose and programme for each group and therefore manages them in the various dispensations according to different principles and covenants (although they also have much in common for there is one God working out one ultimate purpose).

Thus dispensationalism distinguishes between PERIODS and PEOPLES, being careful to discern the differing times, seasons and peoples of God. When we study a passage, we should consider of which dispensation and to which people it is speaking. This will gives us a clearer understanding of scripture. This is particularly important in studying prophecy. Each dispensation has its distinctive characteristics by which it can be recognised.

These Dispensations are mostly self-evident from the Bible:

The First 2000 Years of Redemption History (the Age of the Gentiles).
*Kairos: CREATION (Gen1) and the Edenic Covenant (Gen 1:28-30, 2:15-17).

1. The Dispensation of INNOCENCE (Genesis 2). 40 days.

*Kairos: The FALL and the resulting CURSE upon Adam (Genesis 3:14-19).

2. The Dispensation of CONSCIENCE (Genesis 4-6). 1600 years.

*Kairos: The FLOOD and the NOAHIC COVENANT (Genesis 7:1-9:17).

3. The Dispensation of HUMAN GOVERNMENT (Genesis 9-11). 400 years.

*Kairos: The ABRAHAMIC COVENANT (introduced in Genesis 12:1-3 and developed in Gen15:1-21, 17:1-21, 26:2-5, 28:10-17). It is the mother of all the later covenants, through which God moved His plans of redemption and kingdom forward. The covenants before this were made to all mankind, but now God focuses on Abraham and His seed.

The Second 2000 Years of Redemption History (the Age of Israel).

4. The Dispensation of PROMISE (Genesis 12 - Exodus 11). 500 years.

*Kairos: The EXODUS and the MOSAIC COVENANT (Exodus-Deuteronomy). This covenant through Moses was given purely to Israel, as a temporary covenant in preparation for the eternal new-covenant that Christ would bring.

5. The Dispensation of the LAW (Numbers - end of the O.T). 1500 years. (AD 26-33: **The Time of Messiah -** the time of the ministry of John the Baptist and Jesus Christ was a special 7 years that was to be the last 7 years of the Age of Israel. In this transitional time, Christ fulfilled the Old-Covenant and founded the New-Covenant in its place. Due to Israel's rejection of Messiah, these last 7 years of the Age of Israel were cancelled and rerun as the Tribulation. This is the origin of the Tribulation).

*Kairos: The FIRST COMING of CHRIST (His Death, Resurrection and establishment of the NEW-COVENANT in AD 33 (see the Gospels).

The Third 2000 Years of Redemption History (The Church-Age).

6. The Dispensation of the CHURCH (the Mystery). 2000 years. (Acts & Epistles & Revelation 2,3)

*Kairos: The RAPTURE (John 14:1-3, 1Corinthians15:50-57, 1Thess 4:13-18).

(The TRIBULATION. A 7 year period of world-wide judgement (Revelation 4-18). This is the rerun of the last 7 years of the Age of Israel (AD26-33).

*Kairos: The Second Coming of CHRIST (Revelation 19).

The Final 1000 Years of Redemption History (the Age of Christ).

7. The Dispensation of the MILLENNIUM (the Messianic Age, 1000 years) (Revelation 20:1-6)

*Kairos: Gog & Magog. Great White Throne. The New Creation (Rev 20:7-15).

8. Eternity. The Dispensation of the FULLNESS OF TIMES (Eph1:10,KJV).

God's purpose for the dispensations is described in Acts 17:26-28:

"He has made from one blood every nation of men to dwell on all the face

of the earth, and has determined <u>their preappointed times</u> and the boundaries of their dwellings, <u>so that they should seek the Lord</u>, in the hope that they might grope for Him <u>and find Him</u>." The dispensational 'times and seasons' are fixed by Father's own authority (Acts1:7), for He is the Planner.

<u>Hebrews 1:1,2</u>: **"God, who at <u>various times and in various ways</u> spoke in time past to the fathers by the prophets** (the different dispensations of the past)**, has <u>in these last days</u> spoken to us by His Son** (the present dispensation of the New-Covenant personally mediated by Jesus Christ) **whom He has appointed heir of all things, through whom also He made the worlds** (literally, **'the ages'** or dispensations).**"** Although God's Word (revelation) has progressed and His adminstration has changed through the Ages, yet the basis of man's salvation and pleasing God in every dispensation is FAITH (see Hebrews 11 which gives examples of believers from all Ages).

Thus dispensationalism helps us to not confuse Israel and the Church and to understand the flow of history from God's viewpoint. It helps us to discern whether prophecies are speaking of the Church-Age, the Tribulation, the Millennium or the Eternal-State or one of the 'Kairos' interventions of God, such as the Second-Coming of Christ.

This book gives a dispensational view of Bible-Prophecy. However, I should point out that some reject dispensationalism out of hand, because some dispensationalists have misused and misapplied it to support false beliefs. We need to separate the baby from the dirty bathwater!

One misuse of dispensationalism is the invention another dispensational break within the Church-Age when the canon of scripture was completed to justify Cessationalism (the belief that the supernatural gifts of the Spirit have now passed away). This has no scriptural basis and has been a source of much unbelief in the Church, blocking the flow of God's supernatural power. Another 'dispensational' error is the relegation of the teaching of Jesus in the Gospels to 'Old-Covenant' teaching (and therefore not applicable to us).

In fact, Jesus was not just fulfilling the Old (Mosaic) Covenant in His life and teaching, but He was also founding the New-Covenant and His teaching is the foundation for the New-Covenant Age, which the apostles built upon.

This is proved by Matthew 28:19,20 where Jesus commands the Church to: **"Go therefore and make disciples of all the nations....teaching them to observe all things that I (Jesus) have commanded you** (as recorded in the Gospels); **and lo, I am with you always, even to the end of the Age** (the Age or Dispensation of the Church)."** This proves that these instructions apply to all believers for the whole of the Church-Age. The Holy-Spirit inspired the apostles to record Jesus' teaching for the Church-Age (John 14:26), and also led them into further truth (the Epistles) that built upon that foundation (John 16:13). Paul deliberately builds his teaching on the teaching of Jesus (see 1Cor 7:10,12). John 14-17 gives the foundational teaching of the New Covenant. Thus the Epistles should be understood as building on the foundation of the revelation of Jesus in His Person, Works and Words as recorded in the Gospels.

PROGRESSIVE REVELATION. Dispensationalism helps us to follow God's progressive revelation to man through history, and to interpret scripture accordingly. God revealed His purposes in time. Therefore His revelation to man grew over time.   Like reading any book, the Bible is best understood by reading from the beginning.   The writer introduces the main themes and develops them, so that some things are unclear early on, but made clearer later on.   Thus the New Testament makes many things clearer that were foreshadowed in the Old-Testament (but without contradiction). The New is in the Old concealed. The Old is in the New revealed. We need the Old to understand the New and vice versa. The New helps helps us greatly in understanding how the Old Testament prophecies are fulfilled, as much (but not all) Old-Testament prophecy is fulfilled in the New.

There are two basic ways of interpreting prophecy corresponding to the two ways of comparing and combining the Old and New Testaments.

1. Dispensationalists see the Bible as built on the foundation of the Old Testament and so we start there - reading it as it was written. Of course many things will be unclear and some completely hidden in the Old-Testament. But the main themes should be clear. God, just like the writer of a novel, reveals Himself progressively; and so to understand His Book rightly, we must read it from the beginning and start with the Old Testament prophets. They saw that all history was moving towards the Coming of the Messiah as the King of Kings who would personally set up a literal, visible and political Kingdom of God on earth in great power and glory (the Messianic Kingdom). They predicted that the Messiah (the Son of David) would reign over the earth from Jerusalem with Israel exalted among the nations. This belief is called Pre-Millennialism (see Key 3) and upholds a literal interpretation of the prophetic Scriptures. Thus dispensationalists accept the prophetic scenario that the Old-Testament presents and expects the New Testament revelation to fit within that. The New is properly understood by fitting it upon the Old Testament foundation. It may make many things clear that were unclear and reveal some completely new things, but it does not nullify the Old Testament truth. Now in reading the Bible we often tell people to start with the New because it's an easier way to get started, but if we are to officially interpret it, like any book, we should follow and accept its thought from the beginning.

2. By emphasising that the New clarifies the Old, some say we must reinterpret and spiritualise the Old to fit it into the New, resulting in breaking the key rule of literal interpretation. So, since Christ established the Church instead of the Messianic Kingdom they say the Church fulfils those prophecies and God will not establish this Kingdom, even though the New-Testament also clearly teaches it (Rev20). They say that the New-Testament emphasis on the Church as God's covenant people means we should rewrite Old Testament references to Israel and the Kingdom as applying to the Church. But, would you take this approach in reading a novel? Just because later chapters may bring new peviously unseen developments and reveal new meanings in earlier chapters, does not allow you to rewrite the earlier chapters. They must stand.

Key 3: Pre-Millennialism

One immediate and classic consequence of a literal interpretation of prophecy is PRE-MILLENNIALISM, which teaches that King Jesus will return to earth at His Second-Coming (Revelation 19) and then personally establish His Kingdom on earth, over which He will reign as King of kings, in fulfillment of the Old-Testament Prophets, and this earthly Messianic Kingdom will last for 1,000 years (Revelation 20), before time moves into eternity. If you are not Pre-millennial then that immediately shows you do not take prophecy literally.

Thus, the Second Coming of Christ comes immediately before the Millennium. This is PRE-MILLENNIALISM.

To deny this requires rejecting a literal interpretation of Revelation 19 and 20, as well as many Old-Testament prophecies of the Lord (Messiah) returning to establish His Kingdom on earth. The orthodox Jews understand this, for they explain their rejection of Jesus as the Messiah, by saying that He failed to establish this Kingdom. We shall see why Jesus did not fulfil these prophecies in His First Coming. However, He surely will when He returns the second time. The Old-Testament also predicts that there will be a short time (7 years) of great distress just before the Coming of Messiah (the Tribulation), which the Jews call 'the birth pains of the Messiah.'

The order of events is therefore:
- **The First Coming of Christ**
- **The Present Age**
- **The Tribulation**
- **The Second Coming of Christ**
- **The Millennium.**
- **The Eternal State**

The Book of Revelation gives us a clear sequence of events that agrees with the Old Testament:

1. **The First Coming of Christ** (Revelation 1)
2. **The Present Age** (Revelation 2-3)
3. **The Tribulation** (Revelation 4-18)
4. **The Second Coming of Christ** (Revelation 19)
5. **The Millennium** (Revelation 20).
6. **The Eternal State** (Revelation 21-22).

This gives us our overall framework of Bible prophecy.

WHERE IS HISTORY HEADING? - The Millennium.

2000 AD brought in a new Millennium (1000 years). **Some** see it as a new start, the dawning of a New Age of peace and prosperity, as the nations learn to live together in global unity with a common religion. **Others** see over-population, increasing weather disturbances, earthquakes, pollution, food, water and oil shortages and cannot see how humanity can survive another 40 years.

The Bible has a lot to say about a coming Millennium. It talks about a period of 1000 years that is coming soon (Revelation 20). **There will be righteousness, prosperity and peace under one world-ruler** - JESUS CHRIST, THE LION OF JUDAH! **We are now in the final COUNTDOWN TO THIS MILLENNIUM.**

This book is a detailed look at what is soon to come to pass as history moves to its climax in the 1000-year reign of Christ. We are looking at what the Bible predicts will happen soon!

Mankind has always held a deep hope for a age of peace and justice, with no corruption or poverty.   But man is foolish if he thinks he can establish it himself.   From Nimrod at the Tower of Babel to conquerors like Napoleon and Hitler, men have tried to establish world-wide empires that would bring order for 1000 years.   Communism is motivated by this vision of 1000 years of universal government and peace. The problem is that all these rulers were sinners and were not qualified to rule. It always ends as tyranny.   Through-out history the forces of darkness are in conflict with the Kingdom of God. Both want to establish dominion on earth. Satan's programme is to set up a one-world government and religion and put his man in charge (the antichrist) thus gaining total control.   But GOD IS IN CONTROL.   God foiled this at the Tower of Babel and will again at the Battle of Armageddon.   History is moving towards a great climax where satan's kingdom reaches its fullest outward form (in the Great Tribulation) and God moves to judge and destroy it before all mankind is destroyed.   Then God will establish His King and Kingdom on earth when Jesus Christ comes again.

There is a coming world conqueror and ruler - **KING JESUS!**
He will establish a literal Kingdom of peace on earth. Only the Lord Jesus Christ is able and worthy to rule over the kingdoms of the earth!

THE CONSISTENT VISION OF THE OLD TESTAMENT PROPHETS was that **the future Messiah, the son of David, would rule over this Kingdom:**

"Unto us a child is born, unto us a son is given and the GOVERNMENT (of earth) **shall be upon his shoulder and his name shall be called Wonderful, Counsellor, Mighty God, Everlasting Father** (the Author or Source of Eternal Life), **Prince of Peace ...and of the increase of His government and peace there shall be no end, upon the THRONE OF DAVID** (an earthly throne) **and upon His Kingdom** (an earthly Kingdom)" (Isaiah 9:6,7)

Luke1:31-33 confirms that this refers to Jesus:
"You shall bring forth a son and shall call His name Jesus. He shall be great and shall be called the Son of the Highest and the Lord God shall give to Him the throne of His father David and He shall reign over the

house of Jacob (Israel) **forever."** The Jewish hope from their inspired prophets was the establishment of the Kingdom of God on earth ruled over by the Messiah, from Jerusalem.   This is how they understood these prophecies.

This Kingdom is the focal point of history. All the prophets looked forward to it (Acts 3:21). After speaking on present events and things that God would do, they then always looked beyond these to this Golden Age of peace and glory on earth that Messiah would bring when, **"the knowledge of the Lord would cover the earth as the waters cover the sea"** (Isaiah 2:2-4; 11:6-9; 65:17-25). They understood these prophecies literally, and so should we.

THE NEW TESTAMENT REVELATION of this Age has little to add because so much has already been revealed to us about it in the Old Testament. But one new thing that it does tell us is its duration of 1000 years.

The key passage is Revelation 20:1-7 which agrees with the prophets:
"I saw an angel come down from heaven, having the key of the bottomless pit and a great chain in his hand and he laid hold on the dragon, that old serpent, the devil, and satan, and bound him a 1000 years and cast him into the bottomless pit, and shut him up, and set a seal on him, that he should deceive the nations no more, till the 1000 years should be fulfilled ...and I saw thrones and they sat upon them, and judgment was given to them and I saw the souls of those beheaded for the witness of Jesus, and for the Word of God, who had not worshipped the beast, neither his image, neither had received his mark on their foreheads, or in their hands and they lived and reigned with Christ a 1000 years. But the rest of the dead lived not again until the 1000 years were finished

22

....they shall be priests of God and Christ and shall <u>reign with Him 1000 years</u> and when <u>the 1000 years</u> are expired satan shall be loosed out of his prison." <u>Six times we are told it will be 1000 years!</u>

So we call it the Millennium which means 1,000 years (Latin: mille = 1,000). The Millennium is also called the (Messianic) Kingdom.

The New Testament also refers it as the time when the Kingdom will be restored to Israel (Acts 1:6), the Regeneration of the earth when Christ will sit on His earthly throne and the 12 apostles of the Lamb will sit on 12 thrones judging the 12 Tribes of Israel (Matthew 19:28) and the Times of the Restitution (Restoration) of all things, spoken of by all the prophets (Acts 3:21). The judgements that determine who will enter this Messianic Kingdom (and how believers will be rewarded with different positions of authority in it) are described in Matt 25.

THIS KINGDOM OF GOD IS THE KEY TO PROPHECY.

The Millennium is the climax of prophecy. All history has been flowing like a river toward this destination - the Millennial Sea. Like a woman in pregnancy, the earth has been moving towards the birth of the Kingdom of God upon this planet. As the time gets closer, the birth-pains (disturbances in nature and trouble in the nations) get more intense (Matthew 24:6-8). The word 'sorrows' in Matthew 24:8 is 'birth-pains'. The baby is the Kingdom of God on earth.

Jesus told us to pray: **"Thy kingdom come on earth as it is in heaven."**

To understand prophecy we must understand that all history is moving toward this Age. Thus our view of the Millennium is a touchstone for how we read and understand ALL prophecy. **What we believe about the MILLENNIUM governs our whole viewpoint of prophecy.**

<u>**For the prophets the Millennium was the climax of history**</u> when all the promises of the unconditional covenant with ABRAHAM would be fulfilled.

These promises were three-fold and were expanded in three Covenants:

1. THE PALESTINIAN COVENANT - the promise of NATIONHOOD and much LAND to Israel (from the Nile to the Euphrates).

2. THE DAVIDIC COVENANT - the promise of a Kingdom and King (a son of David of whom Solomon was a type) who would rule the nations with a rod of iron from David's throne in Jerusalem.

3. THE NEW COVENANT (Jeremiah 31:31-34) provided the new-birth
and every spiritual blessing in abundance for Israel.

The Millennium is crucial because it is the high point and focal point of prophecy
and all history is moving toward the time when God will literally and completely
fulfil all His promises and covenants.   As understanding CREATION is essential
because it is the ORIGIN of all history, so understanding the MILLENNIAL
KINGDOM is essential because it is where all history is flowing towards.
This is why it was one of the main revelations of the Jewish prophets
- it is foundational to all prophecy.

**Thus Israel has always looked forward to the GOLDEN MESSIANIC AGE
- when the Son of David rules upon the earth with Israel as head nation.**

But, many Christians do not believe this will happen. They think these promises
to Israel are to be spiritualised and applied to the Church (REPLACEMENT
THEOLOGY).   They say God has no special role for Israel as a nation any more
- for they say: 'Now, the Church is Israel.' NO, NO, NO!   This is a serious
error which the apostle Paul specifically warns against (see Romans 11).
It changes the clear meaning of the prophets who were speaking about Israel,
and it makes GOD a LIAR. God made promises to Israel and is not free to say,
'I really didn't mean Israel, I meant another group of people.'   When you start
spiritualising scripture there is no control to stop you making it mean whatever
you want it to mean. We must take Scripture at its plain meaning.

Now through our union with Christ (the seed of Abraham) we come into all the
blessings of the New Covenant (Galatians 3:26), but this does not contradict the
fact that God will also bring the whole nation of Israel into the New Covenant
(Jeremiah 31:31-34).   The New Testament always keeps a clear distinction
between Israel and the Church (Romans 9-11). God has distinct programmes
for both peoples. God's unconditional promises and covenants to Israel must be
all fulfilled and indeed they will be in the Millennium. His faithfulness requires it.

24

THE THREE VIEWS ON THE MILLENNIUM

1. PRE-MILLENNIUM (Jesus establishes the Millennium, when He comes again)

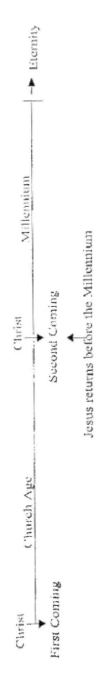

Christ — Church Age — Second Coming — Millennium — Eternity

First Coming

Jesus returns before the Millennium

2. POST-MILLENNIUM (The Church Establishes God's Kingdom on Earth)

Christ — Church Age — Millennium — Second Coming — Eternity

First Coming

The Church Establishes God's Kingdom on Earth

3. A – MILLENNIUM (There will be no literal kingdom of God (Millennium) on earth)

Christ — Church Age — Second Coming — Eternity

First Coming

You are in one of three main Prophetic Camps:

1. PRE-MILLENNIALISM. 'Pre' means 'before'. The Second Coming of Christ marks the beginning of the Millennium. <u>Jesus Christ alone will return before the Millennium to personally establish the promised Kingdom of God on earth and rule over it from Jerusalem, fulfilling the clear vision of the Old-Testament prophets</u>. The world will become more and more ungodly until the Lord comes in power and glory and begins to reign. Only after the 1,000 years will the end come, and Eternity begin. So, Christ could return at any time.
This viewpoint comes directly from taking prophecy literally and so it declares that God has promised Israel a future. The early Church believed this way. <u>This viewpoint is developed in this Book</u>. The other two views have to spiritualise much prophecy and apply Israel's promises to the Church.

<u>A clear proof for the Pre-Millennial view is in the Book of Revelation</u>.
In Revelation 19, we see the Return (the Second Coming) of Jesus.
Then in Revelation 20, we see the 1000 year Kingdom He establishes as a result. The other two views have a difficult time interpreting Revelation 19 and 20. If you understand these chapters literally then you will tend to interpret all prophecy in it's plain meaning.

If you are Pre-Millennial, then you take the prophetic scripture literally which leads to reading scripture in a completely different way from a person who does not believe in a literal Millennial Kingdom on earth. Pre-Millennialism actually leads to a systematic way of interpreting the Bible which has consequences beyond just the prophetic scriptures. It is a crucial issue.

Sadly, during Church history the Church moved away from Pre-Millennialism and so it is not the belief of the majority of the Church world.

2. POST-MILLENNIALISM "Post' means 'after'. Like Pre-Millennialists they believe in a literal kingdom of God that will dominate the earth but this Kingdom is to be established by the Church, not by Christ Himself. Moreover, Christ will not be physically present to personally reign on earth but the Church will rule the world (Israel has no special place).   The Second Coming of Christ will be after this Millennial Kingdom set up by the Church. The Church will 'win' the world making it totally Christian, bringing in 1,000 years of peace (the Millennium, the Kingdom of God on earth).   Then, Christ returns after the Millennium (reversing Revelation 19 and 20). So Christ's Return is probably at least 1,000 years away and is not imminent. Things are believed to be getting better in the world.   It is an exciting vision for the Church but is unbiblical.   It ignores all the Biblical prophecy describing the increase of evil in the world, right up to the Second Coming. It only really developed with JONATHAN EDWARDS (1639-1716) and DANIEL WHITBY (1638 - 1725). It was most popular during the 19th century at the height of the British Empire. But it is not so popular now as the events of the 20th century have made it unrealistic.   It almost died out when the First World War started but since 1945 it has had an increase. It tends to turn the Church from evangelism to politics and social action. Restorationism and Dominion Theology belong in this camp.   The problem with this view is that it over-glorifies the Church at the expense of Christ.   He alone can and will establish the Kingdom. Only Jesus can make the massive world-changes required for the promised Kingdom on earth. It needs the personal presence of the Prince of Peace to establish the Kingdom of peace upon the earth!

3. A-MILLENNIALISM is the general view in the historic (Protestant and Catholic) denominational churches. 'A' is Greek for 'no' or 'without'.
They do not believe that there will a literal 1,000 year Kingdom on earth, but that the Church is the Kingdom.   They redefine the promised Kingdom to be a spiritual Kingdom - rather than a literal Kingdom that will dominate the earth in its politics, religion and economics.   Jesus will simply return and take us to Heaven but He will have no earthly kingdom.   The 1,000 years of Revelation 20 is just picture language for the Church-Age. So, satan is bound now (although they have to say he is on a long leash!).   All prophecy of the Millennium or the Kingdom are but spiritual pictures of the Church or the Eternal State. For example: ***'the wolf shall lie down with the lamb'*** (Isaiah 11:6) is spiritualised

and applied to the Church, meaning that aggressive people will get on with mild people in the Church. But we have no right to spiritualise scripture! We should take its obvious meaning. They believe that Christ's Second Coming is after the Church, and it brings in the Final Judgement and Eternal State. Christ could come at any time. Well known Amillennialists include Augustine, Luther, Calvin, Bishop Wordsworth, Kuyper, Berkhof, Hendrickson, Malcolm Smith.

It is generally agreed that a literal interpretation of the prophets leads to PRE-MILLENNIALISM. They spoke of God moving history toward a Golden Messianic Age. The MESSIAH would come, destroy evil and judge the earth and reign on earth with Israel exalted as a nation. They spoke of a literal Kingdom of God ON EARTH. Thus Israel including the Jews of Jesus' day were looking for this King.

The History of Prophetic Interpretation.

1. **It is agreed that the Old Testament believers, the Jews of Jesus day, the apostles, the early Church for the first three or four centuries interpreted the prophets literally and was entirely Pre-Millennial**. The supporters in the first century are named as: Andrew, Peter, Philip, Thomas, John, James, Matthew, Aristo and John the Presbyter (all are named as such by Papias). From 100-200 AD the list includes Clement of Rome, Barnabus, Ignatius, Polycarp and Papias (both disciples of John). From 200-300AD are Pothinus, Justin Martyr, Melito, Tatian, Irenaeus, Tertullian, Hippolytus, Apollinaris. Up to 300 AD not one opponent can be named. From 300-400 AD at least seven other supporters can be named including Cyprian and Lactantius. At this time Origen marks the beginning of opposition to Pre-Millennialism. It then waned until the present day when it has seen a revival in Bible-believing churches.

2. **AUGUSTINE.** **PHILO** of Alexandria (30BC - 40AD) introduced allegorical interpretation in order to harmonise scripture with Greek Philosophy. He influenced **ORIGEN** of Alexandria (185AD - 254AD) who developed allegory in the Church. Then **AUGUSTINE** rejected the literal interpretation of scripture seeing the prophecies about Israel as applying spiritually to the Church. Through **Augustine** this became the official position at the same time that the Church became ecclesiastical and authoritarian. So this view became entrenched. **Thus it was believed there would be no LITERAL MILLENNIUM = A-MILLENNIALISM.** AUGUSTINE became the main exponent of this view in his book 'The City of God'.

This view makes no promises except that Jesus returns and brings in eternity (the 1000 years of Revelation 20 with satan bound is now). Augustine thought the Church-Age would end by 1000 AD and so there was Millennial fever then! When this didn't happen, it opened the way for **POST-MILLENNIALISM.** The explanations were that this age was of indefinite length or that the binding of satan for 1000 years might start sometime in the Church-Age. Both opened the door to the thought that the Church (not Christ) would bind satan and establish a literal Kingdom of God on earth. Then Christ would return after 1000 years of Christian peace. (This is a recent interpretation, popular at end of the 19th century but not so much now).
Well known Postmillennialists are Charles Hodge, A.Strong, B.B. Warfield, Gresham Machen, Rushdoony, Gary North and Ern Baxter.

3. The CATHOLIC CHURCH throughout the Dark Ages took Augustine's attitude to scripture. If they did not like or understand the literal meaning of a scripture they spiritualised it and gave it the interpretation they wanted. The principle of allegory gave the Church freedom to spiritualise which in turn reduced the authority of scripture. They could now bend scripture to fit with new traditions that increased the Church's authority and power. Scripture was not read literally and thus only the Church could interpret it properly and the people could not do so for themselves.

4. THE REFORMATION. The root of the **REFORMERS'** work was to bring the Church back to a LITERAL interpretation of scripture - that it should be read according to the laws of grammar: **"The true meaning of scripture is the natural and obvious meaning and let us embrace and abide by it resolutely."** - Calvin. This enabled them to rediscover the true doctrine of salvation. It also meant that the Bible could be read and interpreted by all and this drove the translation of scripture from Latin to our own languages. **But in the area of prophecy, the historic Protestant churches did not move away from AUGUSTINE and CATHOLICISM. A-MILLENNIALISM** is still the view of most in the historic churches although it does not explain Revelation 19 and 20.

5. PRE-MILLENNIALISM and the literal interpretation of prophecy has seen a revival in the present day. Most Pentecostal and Independent Bible-Believers are Pre-Millennial. John Milton, John Wesley, Dean Alford, L.S.Chafer, Darby, Schofield, Hal Lindsey (who wrote the 'Late Great Planet Earth'), Merrill Unger, Charles Ryrie, John Walvoord, Dwight Pentecost, Roger Price, Derek Prince, David Pawson and Arnold Fruchtenbaum are well-known Pre-Millennialists today.

Key 4: Israel and the Church

The distinct identity of ISRAEL and THE CHURCH follows from a literal interpretation of scripture. 'Israel' means Israel, and the 'the Church' means the Church! We have seen that the distinction between Israel and the Church is a fundamental part of dispensationalism, but it has become blurred in many systems of theology which talk about the Church replacing Israel and becoming 'spiritual Israel'. When allegorisation came into Church history through Justin Martyr, Irenaeus, Origen and Augustine, the Church developed a false doctrine that it had replaced Israel as God's covenant people, that it now fulfils God's promises to Israel, and was to be known as 'the New Israel' or 'Spiritual Israel'. Because Israel was unfaithful to God, God changed His mind and reapplied His promises to Israel to the Church, even though they were unconditional. This casts doubts upon God's faithfulness. Paul rejects this view in Romans 3:3,4:

"What if some did not believe? shall their unbelief make the faith of God without effect? God forbid: yea, let God be true, but every man a liar."

God will still be faithful to His promises to Israel. We shall see that the Bible, and especially the New-Testament, gives no support to this way of thinking. Instead we see that there are two distinct chosen People of God (Israel and the Church) and that God has a distinct plan and programme for each group that He is working out. Israel's national rebirth (1948) confirms she is still in God's program.

This self-evident distinction is very clear in the New Testament:

1. "Give no offence either (1) to the Jews (Israel) **or (2) to the Greeks** (the Gentiles) **or (3) to the Church of God"** (1Corinthians 10:32).
In this important New Testament scripture Paul distinguishes three groups of people. To rightly understand prophecy we must do likewise. This means that promises to Israel apply firstly to Israel not the Church.
ISRAEL and the CHURCH are distinct peoples of God whose destiny and prophecies are intertwined. In reading prophecy we need to understand if it relates to Israel or the Church if we are to avoid confusion.

2. The Church is new. National Israel came into existence at the Exodus, but

the Church was newly born at Pentecost AD 33 (Acts2:1-4, 11:15,16)
The Church could not exist until Christ died, for it is built upon the Messiah and His blood. In Matthew 16:18, Jesus announced that He would build a new entity, the Church which was not yet in existence: **"On this Rock I will build My Church, and the gates of Hades shall not prevail against it."**
He then immediately began predicting His death (v21).

Likewise Jesus also predicted the Church in connection with His death in John 10:14-16: **"I am the Good Shepherd; and I know My sheep, and am known by My own. As the Father knows Me, even so I know the Father; and I lay down My life for the sheep. And other sheep I have** (believing Gentiles) **which are not of this fold** (Israel); **them also I must bring, and they will hear My voice; and there will be one Flock** (the Church, made up of believing Jews and Gentiles) **and one Shepherd** (Jesus Christ).**"**

The Church is also called a NEW-Creation in Christ - the one NEW Man: **"So as to create in Himself <u>one New Man</u> from the two** (Jews and Gentiles), **thus making peace"** (Ephesians 2:15). Having talked about both Israel and the Gentiles in v11-14, He distinguishes them both from the New-Man which is comprised of believing members from both. The New-Man is the Body of Christ, the Church (v16) and is built on the basis of Christ's death (v13,14). Therefore Paul sees 3 distinct groups: Israel, the Gentiles and the New-Man in Christ.

Moreover, the Church could not come into being until Christ was raised from the dead, for He is the Head of the Body (the Church) and He only became the Head by virtue of HIs resurrection (Eph1:20-23). Likewise, the Church is called a Temple of God, newly built upon Christ, who, by His resurrection, became the Cornerstone (Matthew 21:42, Ephesians 2:20-22, 1Peter2:4-8, Matthew 16:18). Finally, the Church could only become fully functional after His ascension and the outpouring of the Holy-Spirit on the Day of Pentecost.
<u>Therefore the Church must be a distinct entity from Israel</u>.

3. The Church is called a MYSTERY hidden in God in the Old-Testament and therefore could not be same as Israel (more on this in Part 2).

4. The New-Testament never refers to the Church as Israel, neither does it call believing Gentiles 'spiritual Jews'. There is no such confusion of language. There are 77 references in the New Testament to ISRAEL or ISRAELITE, and the apostles never used 'Israel' as a synonym for 'the Church'. The 'New Israel' is never used. While Israel may be used as a Type of the Church and we can learn from their experiences (1Corinthians 10:11), nevertheless the Church is not Israel.

The word 'Jew' occurs nearly 200 times.   Out of all these, Romans 2:28,29 is the only passage that uses this term is a special sense: **"For he is not a Jew, which is one outwardly; neither is that circumcision, which is outward in the flesh: But he is a Jew, which is one inwardly; and circumcision is that of the heart, in the spirit,**
and not in the letter; whose praise is not of men, but of God."
Paul here plays on the meaning of Jew, which from Judah means 'praise'. He is saying that to be a true Jew it is not enough to be one outwardly but also inwardly so that he has the praise of God.   Paul is not extending the use of Jew to Gentiles, rather he is restricting its use to believing Jews. We use the word 'Christian' in the same special way sometimes: *'If you were a true Christian, you would turn the other cheek.'*   Revelation 2:9 and 3:9 also uses 'Jew' in this special sense.   These alone among the 200 passages use 'Jew' in its special meaning.   So the normal use of the word 'Jew', which applies to both believing and unbelieving Israelites, has not been replaced.

In the 77 New Testament passages naming 'Israel', nine are quotes from the Old Testament where the meaning of 'Israel' is exactly the same as the Old Testament.   Also 66 of the remaining passages use the word in the normal way.

There remain only 2 passages where 'Israel' is used in a special sense:

1. "Not as though the word of God has taken none effect.
For they are not all Israel, which are of Israel: Neither, because they

are the seed of Abraham, are they all children: but, In Isaac shall thy seed
be called.   That is, they which are the children of the flesh,
these are not the children of God: but the children of the promise are
counted for the seed.   For this is the word of promise, at this time
will I come, and Sarah shall have a son"** (Romans 9:6-9).
Again, Paul is restricting the name 'Israel' to those Jews who have the spiritual
qualification of faith as well as the natural qualification of birth.   Paul is not here
extending the use of Israel to include believing Gentiles.   Elsewhere in this
passage Paul uses Israel in the normal sense of all those physically descended
from Abraham, Isaac and Jacob, including unbelievers (v3-5).

2. The only other passage where 'Israel' is used in a restricted sense is Galatians
6:15,16: **"For in Christ Jesus neither circumcision avails any thing, nor
uncircumcision, but a new creature.   And as many as walk according to
this rule, peace be on them, and mercy, and upon the Israel of God."**

Paul here is referring to two groups of people:
Firstly, there are uncircumcised Gentiles who are new creations.
Secondly, there are circumcised Israelites who have come to faith in Christ -
these are 'The Israel of God'. Paul is saying both are equal in Christ because all
that really matters is the New Birth, not a religious rite. The NIV has wrongly
changed "**and** upon the Israel of God" to "**even** the Israel of God" because of
the widespread teaching that all believers are 'the Israel of God' or 'spiritual
Israel.' However the Greek word **'kai'** almost always means 'and' not 'even'.
Thus the two groups with different backgrounds are one in Christ.

Confirming the fact that the New Testament does not use 'Israel' as a name for
the Church, there are passages where Israel denotes Jews who rejected Jesus
and so are certainly not the Church: **"What then? Israel has not obtained that
what it seeks; but the elect have obtained it, and the rest were blinded...I
say then, Have they stumbled that they should fall? God forbid: but rather
through their fall salvation is come unto the Gentiles,
to provoke them to jealousy.   Now if their fall is riches for the world,**

and their failure riches for the <u>Gentiles</u>; how much more their fullness?
For I speak to <u>you Gentiles</u>, inasmuch as I am the apostle of <u>the Gentiles</u>,
I magnify mine office: if by any means I may provoke to jealousy those
who are <u>my flesh</u>, and might save some of them" (Romans 11:7, 11-14).
Paul keeps a consistent contrast between Israelites and Gentiles, even though
the Israelites do not believe and the Gentiles do. So Paul does not use Israel as
a name for believing Gentiles. He actually uses the name 'Israel' to distinguish
them from Gentile believers! **"For I do not desire, brethren, that you should
be ignorant of this mystery, lest you should be wise in your own conceits;
that blindness in part is happened <u>to Israel</u>, until the fullness of
<u>the Gentiles</u> is come in"** (v25). He concludes: **"And so all Israel shall be
saved"** (v26). <u>This cannot mean the Church</u>.

<u>In Romans 9-11</u>, Paul consistently makes a distinction between Israel
and the Gentiles. The idea that the Church (of Gentiles) has become Israel
is foreign and only came in the 2nd Century. Therefore the New Testament
does not change or spiritualise the meaning of 'Israel'. God's promises and
covenants to Israel must be fulfilled literally to Israel. Whatever blessings
the Church enjoys in Christ , they do not nullify the blessings to Israel.
The Church does not fulfil the Old Testament prophecies to Israel.

There is a popular teaching today that God has finished with Israel and
that the Church has permanently replaced Israel as God's people. They say
that now all the promises are fulfilled in the Church which is 'spiritual Israel'.
But notice the present tense used in <u>Romans 9:3-5</u>, showing that God has
certainly not finished with Israel: **"For I could wish that I myself were
accursed from Christ for my brethren, my countrymen according to
the flesh, who are Israelites.   <u>Theirs is</u> the adoption, the glory, the
covenants, the giving of the law, the service of God, and the promises.
<u>Theirs are</u> the fathers and from whom, according to the flesh,
Christ came, Who is over all, the eternally blessed God. Amen."**
"I say then, has God cast away His people? Certainly not!

For I also am an Israelite, of the seed of Abraham, *of* **the tribe of Benjamin. God has not cast away His people whom He foreknew"** (Romans 11:1,2). Israel will stand, not because of her own righteousness, but because she is elect of God (v5,6,28). Her full restoration is predicted in v11-16,23-27,31,32, for ultimately: **"all Israel will be saved"** (v26). **"For the gifts and the calling of God** (upon Israel) **are irrevocable"** (v29). Israel is the only nation with a guaranteed future. She is sure to survive for she has a covenant with God.

Replacement theology comes from abandoning the clear literal interpretation of the Bible. The curse of Genesis 12:3 is upon those who teach it: **"Blessed are those who bless you** (Abraham and his seed). **Cursed are those who curse you** (Israel)." Antisemitism is a clear sign of the working of satan in men's hearts The apostle Paul warns the Church against this error and predicts judgement on those (especially those within Christendom) who lift themselves up against Israel, for God has not finished with her and she is still the apple of His eye.

Romans 11:18-22 is a WARNING to the GENTILE NATIONS to beware of expressing pride over Israel. There is a judgement reserved for those who say that God has rejected Israel forever, that He has finished with Israel as a distictive people of God, that He will not fulfil His Covenants with her,and that the (mostly) Gentile Church has now permanently replaced Israel in God's Plan and Purposes: "(You Gentiles) **do not boast against the** (natural) **branches** (Israel). **But if you do boast, remember that you do not support the root, but the root supports you. You will say then, 'Branches were broken off that I might be grafted in.' Well, because of unbelief they were broken off, and you stand by faith. Do not be haughty, but fear. For if God did not spare the natural branches** (Israel), **He may not spare you** (Gentile nations) **either. Therefore consider the goodness and severity of God: on those who fell, severity; but toward you, goodness, if you continue in His goodness. Otherwise you also will be cut off."**
Here he warns of a future JUDGEMENT and CUTTING OFF of the GENTILE NATIONS for their unbelief in Christ and for their pride over Israel.

Key 5: The Sufferings and the Glory

Let's look at the big picture given to us by the Old Testament and see how the New built upon it. **THE PROPHETS SAW TWO ASPECTS OF MESSIAH'S WORK - His SUFFERINGS and the GLORY that would follow.**

GOD'S KINGDOM and SALVATION PROGRAMMES.

After the angelic rebellion, God's original purpose for man (made in God's image) was to reestablish His **KINGDOM** through man - giving him dominion on earth (Genesis 1:26). When man sinned, God did not change His Kingdom Purpose but He had to also bring in His **SALVATION PROGRAMME.** These two programmes determine God's action in history and the fulfilment of end-time prophecy. God is moving to establish His Kingdom on earth, putting all His enemies under His feet. But first, He must provide salvation for man, or else all mankind would be destroyed as God's enemies. Rather than destroying everything and starting again, God purposed to redeem mankind and reestablish His Kingdom on earth.

Both programmes centred in the **MESSIAH.** The original Messianic prophecy revealed that He would accomplish both purposes: "**I will put enmity between you** (the serpent) **and the woman, and between your seed and her Seed** (Messiah); **He shall bruise** (crush) **your head, and you shall bruise His heel**" (Genesis 3:15). First, this predicts that He would destroy the devil and his Kingdom. Christ's death on the Cross provided the basis for satan's final destruction which is yet to happen when Christ reclaims His full authority in every realm. Second, this predicts that in crushing the serpent's head, He would also suffer bruising in the heel (the serpent's bite). This was also fulfilled on the Cross, where Christ bore a terrible assault of the forces of darkness and received into himself the poison of our sin. He did all this to redeem us from the hand of sin, curse and satan's dominion over us.

This two-fold work of the Messiah was typified by two sons.

As the son of Abraham, He would be like Isaac, the willing sacrifice who would rise from death. As the son of David, He would be like Solomon, a King of glory.

So the New Testament introduces Jesus Christ as:
"the son of David, the son of Abraham" (Matthew 1:1).

He is also represented by two symbolic animals: The LION and LAMB.

Christ is the sacrificial Lamb of God, who takes away the sins of the world (John 1:29, Isa 53:7).   He is also the Lion of Judah (Genesis 49:9,10; Revelation 5:5). As the king of the beasts, the lion represents kingly authority.

Thus, out of Judah would come a Ruler who would rule Israel and the world. These two are related in Revelation 5.   In v5, **'the Lion of the tribe of Judah'**, is introduced, but when John looked at the throne to see Him, He saw a **'Lamb that had been slain'** (v6).   In fact, it was because He suffered as a Lamb that He is worthy of Kingly glory (Phil 2:6-11).   This is stated in v12:

"Worthy is the Lamb who was slain to receive power and riches and wisdom and strength and honour and glory and blessing!"

Before He destroys the kingdom of darkness with wrath (the lion), He suffered the fires of judgement himself to rescue sinners, laying down his life as a lamb.

God prepared the way for this two-fold programme of the Messiah by His Covenants.

(1) His Covenant with ABRAHAM promised the Coming of the Messiah (Christ), the Seed of Abraham () who would bless all nations with salvation. This promise was given more detail through the prophets as they described the **NEW COVENANT -** of salvation, regeneration and abundant spiritual blessings, that He would establish. This required the sacrifice of **the LAMB OF GOD** to take away the sins of the world. God gave Israel the temporary **MOSAIC COVENANT** to reveal their sin and need of salvation and also to show how salvation would be provided.   But Israel sinned and the prophets (God's Covenant-Enforcers) were raised up to point out their sin and God's judgements on sin, and also to point forward to the ONE who would come to SAVE His people from their sin and from their enemies.   He would come and reign - fulfilling all the Covenants, because they were unconditional. (Even in the face of Israel's sin and the Gentile dominance, the prophets declared the fulfilment of the covenants).   God knew the Mosaic (OLD) Covenant would fail to save them from sin - it was given to prepare the way for the NEW Covenant brought in by Christ Himself, which could save all men (Jeremiah 31:31-33).

(2) The DAVIDIC COVENANT promised a King and an everlasting Kingdom. The Son of David (the Lion of Judah) would rule the nations with a rod of iron from David's throne in Jerusalem. His son Solomon was a type of this King and Kingdom. Jesus is the 'Greater than Solomon'.

We can get so involved in SALVATION that we forget that its purpose was to restore man to his original purpose in THE KINGDOM PROGRAMME. Thus, our salvation through Christ brings us into God's Kingdom so that we can rule and reign with Him.   Christ's work on the Cross was essential to establishing His Kingdom on earth, because men must be saved for it even to be populated!   **Thus, Christ first had to come to SUFFER for our SALVATION as the LAMB, before He comes to reestablish His KINGDOM and reign in POWER and GLORY as the LION.**

The Cross and Crown

THE SUFFERINGS and THE GLORY

There were **two streams of Messianic prophecy** corresponding to God's two programmes which gave two very different pictures of the Messiah.

(1) The son of Joseph - the Suffering Servant of Isaiah, dying for our sins. This was a Priestly Messiah who would offer Himself as the sacrifice for our sins, before being raised and exalted as Lord.

(2) The son of David - a Kingly Messiah, a conquering King.

WHAT THE OLD TESTAMENT MAKES CLEAR:

(1) Messiah would come to die for our sins to establish a NEW COVENANT (redemption and spiritual blessings) **- the SUFFERING.**

(2) Messiah would come to reign as King on earth on David's Throne - the GLORY.

How both prophecies can be fulfilled is made perfectly clear in the New Testament. <u>Jesus came the first time as the sacrificial Lamb and will come again as the Lion King.</u> The prophets saw visions of the Messiah coming as the KING (THE LION of JUDAH) and also as a SUFFERING SERVANT dying for our sins and rising again (the sacrificial LAMB OF GOD -see Isaiah 53).

Some Jews found it hard to reconcile these two images and so looked for two Messiahs.   Most just looked for the one they wanted - the King who would conquer and save them from the Romans.   One reason they rejected Jesus is that He had to first fulfil His ministry of saving men from sin but in their self-righteousness they weren't looking for this kind of Saviour (and they didn't like the requirement to repent which was part of receiving this salvation to be ready for the Kingdom).

Only after establishing the New Covenant in His Blood could He establish His Kingdom on earth (or else it would just be an enforced external Kingdom rather than one where God reigned in men's hearts). Only when Israel accepts the New Covenant in Christ, can God set up the King and Kingdom on earth, because it is based upon Israel and the Abrahamic Covenant.

The Jews looked forward to the MESSIANIC AGE, when the Son of David will rule with Israel as the chief nation, and the Abrahamic Covenant would be fulfilled in all three aspects.   But they overlooked the passages speaking of the Suffering Servant. They saw the need for a King to deliver them from the Romans but not to save them from their own sin (they were deceived into thinking they saved themselves by their legalistic obeying of the law - that they didn't need a Saviour).   Thus the nation rejected their King.   They didn't realise it was **"the suffering _then_ the glory"** (Luke24:26; 1 Peter 1:11).   Jesus didn't come as the King they were looking for because first He had to die for our sins. Had He moved as JUDGE, the Jews would be destroyed as well the Gentiles.

A careful reading of the Messianic prophecies makes it clear that the Messiah would **FIRST** have to be born and enter into His ministry of **SUFFERING** and **THEN** later enter His **GLORY** as KING of kings.

Likewise Jesus said: **"O foolish ones, and slow of heart to believe in ALL that the prophets have spoken! Ought not the CHRIST** (the Messiah) **to: (1) have SUFFERED these things and** (then) **(2) to enter into His GLORY?" And beginning at Moses and all the Prophets, He expounded to them in all the Scriptures the things concerning Himself"** (Luke 24:25-27). In one sense Jesus personally entered His glory in His resurrection and ascension, but the public manifestation of His glory awaits His Second-Coming and Messianic Kingdom.   The Jews did not believe ALL that the prophets revealed, for while they looked for the GLORIOUS COMING of the Messiah, they overlooked the prophecies of Him coming first as a Suffering Servant.

"Of this salvation (the New Covenant blessings) **the prophets have inquired and searched carefully, who prophesied of the grace that would come to you, searching WHAT TIME or WHAT KIND OF TIME, the Spirit of Christ who was in them was indicating when He testified beforehand of (1) the SUFFERINGS of CHRIST and (2) the GLORIES that would follow"** (1Peter 1:10,11).

They saw the sufferings of Christ (His First Coming) and the glory of Christ (His Second Coming).   WHAT WAS NOT CLEAR to the prophets was how much time ('WHAT TIME') was between these two Comings and what would happen in that time ('WHAT KIND OF TIME'). **What the prophets saw was like looking at two mountain peaks in the distance**. They saw the FIRST Coming of Christ as the Suffering Saviour and the SECOND Coming of Christ as the Conquering King. But they could not see the Valley (the Church-Age) in-between.

40

The Prophet/Seer   Suffering Messiah   Mystery Age

The prophets could not see the TIME (the valley) in between the two Comings of Christ - that we now know as the Church-Age.
Though they searched, it was a MYSTERY to them; as to HOW LONG ('WHAT TIME') it would be, and exactly what God had planned for that time ('WHAT KIND OF TIME'). So as they described what they saw ahead, their prophecies would often JUMP 2000 years across this GAP!

For example: **"Unto us a child is born, unto us a Son is given...** (2000 years) **.... and the government shall be upon his shoulders..."** (Isaiah 9:6-8).
Taken literally (as the original hearers would have understood it) the second half of the verse is talking of Messiah ruling the government of Israel and the whole earth from David's throne in Jerusalem which is still awaiting fulfilment.
As we shall see shortly, there is a good reason why this time-period (now known as the Church-Age) between the two Advents of Christ was a Mystery.

Therefore, from the Old-Testament Prophets, we have this order of events:
- **THE FIRST COMING OF CHRIST** (the Sufferings)
- **A MYSTERY TIME** (Hidden by God in the Old-Testament time)
- **THE SECOND COMING OF CHRIST** (the Glory)
- **THE MILLENNIUM** (the Messianic Age)

Key 6: The Kingdom Offered

THE TRANSITION from ISRAEL to the CHURCH is the MINISTRY OF JOHN THE BAPTIST and JESUS CHRIST.   One of the biggest problems in prophecy is connecting together the two sides of the jigsaw (Old Testament prophecy on the LEFT HAND and the New Testament Church on the RIGHT HAND) into one big consistent picture. The prophesied Messianic Kingdom was very different to what Christ actually brought in - the Church Age.

One solution to this problem has been to spiritualise Old Testament prophecy, call the church 'spiritual Israel' and say that prophecy was fulfilled in the church, but I reject this approach because it denies the literal interpretation of prophecy. To fit together the two sides of the puzzle we must understand where they join - **the ministry of John the Baptist and Jesus Christ.**

JESUS CAME OFFERING THE KINGDOM TO ISRAEL. Jesus came as the Messiah to Israel. According to the prophets, part of His mission was to SUFFER and die for sin, and the other part was to bring in and rule over the promised Kingdom of GLORY.   He said He came **"to fulfil (all) the law and the prophets"** (Matthew 5:17).   John the Baptist was the forerunner of Christ, preparing the way for the King, announcing His imminent arrival.

Jesus said of John: **"But what did you go out to see? A prophet? Yes, I say to you, and more than a prophet.   For this is he of whom it is written: 'Behold, I send My messenger before Your face, Who will prepare Your way before You.' Assuredly, I say to you, among those born of women there has not risen one greater than John the Baptist; but he who is least in the kingdom of heaven is greater than he. And from the days of John the Baptist until now the Kingdom of Heaven forces itself on men's attention, and the forceful ones lay hold of it. For all the prophets and the law prophesied until John"** (Matthew 11:9-13).

Thus John was the last and greatest in the line of prophets heralding Messiah's Coming.   Moreover, **"All the prophets prophesied unto John",** signifies that he was more than a prophet and was actually the first stage of the Messianic fulfilment of prophecy (Malachi 3:1; Isaiah 40:3). Therefore the ministry of Jesus and His presentation of Himself as the Messiah officially began with the ministry of John. The Gospels confirm this. The days of John brought in a sudden change of relationship with the Kingdom of God.

Both John and Jesus came saying: **"Repent and believe the Gospel for the Kingdom of God is at Hand"** (Matthew 3:1, 4:17,10:5-7). In other words Jesus was ready to establish the literal Kingdom of God on earth, as prophesied, in AD 33. It was being offered to Israel on condition that the Nation receive Him as Messiah. To be consistent with Old Testament prophecy, Jesus had to be offering them the Messianic Kingdom. The Jews would naturally have understood this to be the Kingdom the prophets had promised the Messiah would bring. John the Baptist expected Him to establish this Kingdom (Matthew 11:3). At His Triumphal Entry the Jews were clearly expecting this Kingdom:
"Then those who went before and those who followed cried out, saying: "Hosanna! Blessed is He who comes in the name of the LORD!' Blessed is the kingdom of our father David that comes in the Name of the Lord! Hosanna in the highest!" (Mark 11:9,10).

Jesus never said anything to correct this understanding. If He was not really offering israel the Messianic-Kingdom, but just talking spiritually, He would have been deceiving them. Both John and Jesus were announcing that the promised Messianic Kingdom was at hand. However, it was also clear that Israel was not spiritually ready for it. They needed to repent and believe on and receive Christ as their King. Thus John's ministry was to prepare Israel, so that when Jesus appeared they would receive Him as their King and thus the Kingdom would be established. (You can't have a Kingdom without a King and willing subjects).

In Acts 1:6, after the Resurrection, the disciples still expected Jesus to establish this Kingdom in fulfilment of God's covenant promises to Israel: **"They asked Him: "Lord will You at this time restore the** (Messianic) **Kingdom to Israel?"** This proves that Jesus had not taught them that there would not be such a

Kingdom. The only issue was its timing. Jesus answer confirms this:

"And He said to them, "It is not for you to know times ('chronos') **or seasons** ('kairos') **which the Father has put in His own authority"** (v7).

Although Jesus was ready to establish the Kingdom, Israel was not yet ready to receive it. When Jesus spoke these words, Israel was still in the time of decision over Christ, and so He could not clearly reveal to them the timing of the Messianic-Kingdom, for He wanted them to continue to make the offer to Israel for a time. (Of course, we now have much more knowledge of the Father's 'times and seasons'). Jesus knew, however, that Israel would reject Him, and so He prepared His disciples for their Mission in the coming Church-Age:

"But you shall receive power when the Holy Spirit has come upon you; and you shall be witnesses to Me in Jerusalem, and in all Judea and Samaria, and to the end of the earth" (v8).

Israel's unbelief meant the Messianic Kingdom was delayed, but delay is not denial. Instead of establishing this Kingdom, He would first establish a new mystery-dispensation, with a new programme and people of God. Then, after-wards the Kingdom must be established to fulfil the covenants and prophecies.

The condition of Israel over the last 2000 years up to the present day is perfectly explained and described by the Bible. The mystery of Israel to many is both her suffering and existance. Why she has suffered so much, and how she has continued to survive as a nation? As God's elect covenant people, whatever happens she can never be destroyed. But because of her rejection of Messiah, instead of receiving the Kingdom she came under Divine discipline and as a result was scattered to the nations and has suffered greatly (Luke 21:21-24). Despite her unbelief, God has not finished with her, and her discipline is only for a certain time, after which she will be restored. In fulfillment of the many prophecies that she must be regathered to her Land before the end of the age, Israel was miraculously reborn in 1948. God did this in preparation for the Tribulation, which requires Israel to be back in the Land. In this future time, she will face her greatest ever suffering, but God's purpose is to have His final dealings with her to restore her to fellowship and faith, so that by the end of the Tribulation, she will repent and receive Jesus (Yeshua) as her Messiah and call upon Him for salvation. He will then save Israel from destruction at His 2nd Coming, and establish His Kingdom, with Israel fully restored as chief nation. Thus, Israel's sufferings (past, present and future) and the origin and purpose of the Tribulation are explained by Israel's original rejection of the King and Kingdom.

Key 7: The Kingdom Rejected and Postponed.

THE KINGDOM WAS POSTPONED 2000 years because Israel rejected Jesus as their Messiah-King and the New Covenant He offered them in His Blood.

This is not well-known, but understanding this is essential for harmonising Old-Testament prophecy with the New-Testament.

To be consistent with Old Testament prophecy, Jesus offered Israel the Kingdom. This was not fulfilled by the spiritual Kingdom that Jesus actually established through the Church. **So, clearly the literal Kingdom was not established. Rather it was postponed and God inserted an Age which \had been a Mystery hidden in God** (which as we shall see is the teaching of the New Testament). If the Messianic Kingdom was not postponed, then the spiritual Kingdom of the Church-Age that Jesus brought must be the fulfilment of the prophets but this was not what the prophets literally predicted - and we have a major problem!

Why was the Kingdom postponed? It is clear from reading the Gospels that although many individuals received Christ, Israel as a nation (because of her leaders) rejected Him, despite the many proofs He gave them. **"He came to His own, and His own** (ISRAEL) **did not receive Him. But as many as received Him, to them He gave the right to become children of God, to those who believe in His name"** (John 1:11,12).

If Israel had accepted Jesus as their King, He would have been able to establish the Kingdom that very year (A.D.33). However, because they rejected Him, the Kingdom was postponed for 2000 years. Because that generation rejected Him as their King, saying 'we will have no King but Caesar', God rejected them from possessing the Kingdom. It did not mean that the Kingdom would never be established because the Kingdom is based on God's unconditional promises and Covenant with Abraham. It just meant that Christ's generation could not receive it. It was delay not denial.

After describing how Israel had rejected Him, Jesus said: **"The Kingdom of God shall be taken from you and given to a people** (a future generation) **bringing forth the fruits of it"** (a people who will be spiritually qualified to possess the Kingdom) (Matthew 21:43).   This postponement is like Israel's failure to possess the promised land (a type of the Kingdom) through unbelief. They received salvation through the Blood of the Passover Lamb and could have possessed the land the same year but because of unbelief there was a delay of 40 years wandering in the wilderness before a new generation could enter in.   Likewise, the true Passover Lamb was slain in AD33 and had Israel believed she could have possessed the Kingdom that same year but instead she has been wandering in the wilderness of the nations for 2000 years (40 Jubilees!) because of unbelief, but will soon possess the promised Kingdom.

Jesus asked for faith and repentance from Israel in preparation for the Kingdom. John and Jesus came with the message: **"Repent, and believe the Gospel...for the Kingdom of God is at Hand"** (Mark 1:15).   Notice that to possess the Kingdom offered to them, they needed to repent and believe in the Messiah.   To be qualified to enter the Kingdom, they needed to be regenerated and receive forgiveness of sins through the New Covenant in the blood of Christ. (When Christ returns there will be judgments on the living Jews and Gentiles and only believers will be allowed to enter the Kingdom).

For the Kingdom to be established, Israel had to receive Christ and be made spiritually qualified.   The promised Kingdom is based on God's Covenant with Israel. As it is centred on Israel, it cannot be established without her co-operation.   Therefore, Jesus will only return the second time to establish the Kingdom when Israel repents and receives Him as their Messiah:
"O Jerusalem, Jerusalem, the one who kills the prophets and stones those who are sent to her! How often I wanted to gather your children together, as a hen gathers her chicks under her wings, but you were not willing! See! Your house is left to you desolate; for I say to you, you shall see Me no more till you say, 'Blessed is He who comes in the name of the LORD!'" (Matthew 23:37-39).

In the Messianic Kingdom, God will fulfil the whole Abrahamic Covenant with Israel.

This involves: **1. NATIONHOOD and LAND** (The Palestinian Covenant)
2. AN EVERLASTING KING and KINGDOM (The Davidic Covenant)
3. ABUNDANT SPIRITUAL LIFE and BLESSINGS (The New Covenant).

Before Christ, the New Covenant was not made, only promised (Jer31:31-34). God prepared them for the eternal NEW Covenant (in the Blood of God) by giving them a temporary Old Covenant (in the blood of animals).   Israel accepted Moses as the mediator of the OLD COVENANT and so the nation entered into it at Mount Sinai on the day of PENTECOST and Moses was to lead them in to possess the land (Kingdom).   Likewise, JESUS came as **'the prophet like unto Moses'** (Deuteronomy 18:15-19) whom they were to obey as the Mediator of the New Covenant and He would lead them in to possess the Kingdom. If they had accepted Him and His Covenant, Israel as a nation would have entered into the NEW COVENANT on the Day of PENTECOST and they would have had the Kingdom that same year. This would have replaced the OLD Mosaic Covenant in providing forgiveness and spiritual blessing. But they rejected Christ so the offer of the Kingdom was postponed and meanwhile the Church was grafted into Christ and enjoys the blessings of the New Covenant.   In the future, Israel as a nation will enter the New Covenant and be saved and be an exalted nation in the Kingdom Millennium and all God's promises to her will be fulfilled.

Now we can understand the reason that this present period of time (and the Church) could not be clearly revealed in the Old Testament

(although we can now look back and see the Church in some of the Typology of the Old-Testament, it is not mentioned plainly and directly for God was keeping it as a mystery to be revealed in due time). The Messianic Kingdom could not be established until Israel accepted the KING and the NEW COVENANT He brought. This spiritual requirement was necessary for them to enter the Kingdom and for the Kingdom to enter them, but they chose to hold to the OLD COVENANT (the two are mutually exclusive).

Jesus came (1) to SAVE and establish the NEW Covenant in His Blood and (2) to bring in the KINGDOM as King of the Jews. However, Israel had to first receive Him for the latter to be possible. He proclaimed the Kingdom at hand and Himself as their King (see Matthew's Gospel) and if the nation had ACCEPTED Him, the KINGDOM would have been established then. But they REJECTED the offer (and God knew they would). **But it was a genuine offer.** If God had made it clear in advance that they would reject it and that there would be a 2000-year Church Age, then it would not have been a genuine offer. Thus this Church Age was a mystery that God could only start revealing through Jesus and His apostles when it was clear that Israel was rejecting Christ.

With this Key, we can harmonise Old Testament prophecy with the New Testament and do full justice to both (fitting together the two halves of the jigsaw). The prophecies of the Messianic Age are not fulfilled by the Church, but will be fulfilled literally when Jesus returns. The Messianic Age was postponed because Israel was not ready and meanwhile the Church, a Mystery hidden in God, was introduced so that salvation might go to the Gentiles. The Church receives all the spiritual blessings of the New Covenant which the prophets had predicted for the Messianic Age:
"the powers of the age to come" (Hebrews 6:5)

In accepting all the glorious things the New Testament says about the Church, we must not throw away all the great things God says He will do for Israel. However important the Church is, we are only part of God's overall plan. God will fulfil His plan for Israel according to the prophets and His plan for the Church according to the apostles.

Israel's Rejection of Jesus as King and God's response is clearly shown in the Gospels and Acts.

In particular it is a major theme of Matthew's Gospel which presents Jesus as the prophesied Messianic King.

1. Jesus' Early Ministry to Israel. He presented Himself to Israel as

their King claiming to be the Messiah, announcing that the Kingdom
was at hand, and proving this by many miracles (Matthew 1:1-11:1).
Thus the Kingdom was ready to be manifested if Israel would receive it.

2. Opposition. He came against increasing opposition and rejection by

Israel's leaders (Matthew 11:2-16:12).   After 2 years of ministry, it was
becoming clear that Israel's leaders were rejecting Him. This came to a head in
Matthew 12 when He performed a Messianic miracle (a miracle the Jews knew
only Messiah could perform). In order to explain this, the leaders accused Him
of being possessed by satan rather than by God's Spirit (v24). He told them that
this miracle was by the Holy Spirit: **"If I cast out demons by the Spirit of God,
surely the Kingdom of God has come upon you"** (v28). He warned them of
the consequences of rejecting the witness of the Holy Spirit to the Person of
Christ. He said if they reject Him (and His salvation), they could not be forgiven
(v31,32).   He was warning that generation of Israel that if they rejected Jesus as
their Messiah, they would commit an unforgivable sin and come under judgement

He said He would give them one more Messianic sign to prove who He was
- the sign of Jonah - his resurrection from the dead after three days:
"**Then some of the scribes and Pharisees answered, saying,
"Teacher, we want to see a sign from You." But He answered them,
"An evil and adulterous generation seeks after a sign, and no sign will
be given to it except the sign of the prophet Jonah. For as Jonah was
3 days and 3 nights in the belly of the great fish, so will the Son of Man
be 3 days and 3 nights in the heart of the earth"** (v38-40 - also in 16:1-4).
Jesus compared Himself with Jonah (a Type of Christ) - who died and rose again
after three days with acid scars from the belly of the great fish as proof.   This
miraculous sign confirmed His message and Ninevah believed, repented and
were spared from judgement after Jonah was 40 days with them. In the same
way, the death and resurrection of Jesus after 3 days (with the marks
in His body as proof) was His greatest sign to Israel (confirming His claims).

He too was present with Israel 40 days after this, but they still rejected Him. As a result, rather than Israel inheriting the Kingdom, judgement fell upon her instead. By now Jesus knew that Israel would reject Him:

"The men of Nineveh will rise up in the judgement with this generation and condemn it, because they repented at the preaching of Jonah; and indeed a greater than Jonah is here. The queen of the South will rise up in the judgement with this generation and condemn it, for she came from the ends of the earth to hear the wisdom of Solomon; and indeed a greater than Solomon is here" (v41,42).

Finally, Jesus warned Israel again of the consequences of rejecting Him through a Parable: **"When an unclean spirit goes out of a man, he goes through dry places, seeking rest, and finds none. Then he says, `I will return to my house from which I came.' And when he comes, he finds it empty, swept, and put in order. Then he goes and takes with him seven other spirits more wicked than himself, and they enter and dwell there; and the last state of that man is worse than the first. So shall it also be with this wicked generation"** (Matthew 12:43-45). The House of Israel was cleansed through the ministry of John the Baptist in preparation for Jesus to come in and rule as the Messiah. However they rejected Him and the House remained empty. As a result Israel will be invaded and great evil will come upon her in that same generation (fulfilled in AD70 when the Romans invaded and destroyed Jerusalem and burnt the Temple, scattering her to the nations).

3. The Mystery Kingdom Revealed.

This was a turning point for Jesus' ministry. He began preparing the disciples for the NEW dispensation - for what lay ahead after His death and resurrection -THE REVELATION OF THE MYSTERY. (It was so radical that they were not ready for the full revelation which would be given after the resurrection, especially through the Apostle Paul - John 16:12,13). So in Matthew 12:46-50 and Matthew 13, Jesus gave them new teaching in Parables which was the first revelation of the Mystery Kingdom (Church Age) that he would introduce instead of the Messianic Kingdom, because it was now clear Israel was rejecting His offer.   We study these parables in detail later in this book.   They were a form of teaching which allowed Jesus to reveal the Mystery to His disciples while keeping the unbelieving leaders in the dark.   This was necessary because Israel had not yet made a final decision and God had not yet cut her off. This is studied in detail in Part 2.

4. When did God cut Israel off?

Some believe Israel was cut off at this time (before the Cross), but

(1) They first had to be given and reject the sign of Jonah (the raising of Jesus Christ after three days in the heart of the earth - Matthew 12:28-32). This was the greatest Messianic sign which would remove all excuse.

(2) The unforgivable sin of rejecting the witness of the Holy Spirit was not complete until Pentecost and the outpouring of the Spirit.

(3) This is confirmed by the fact that in Acts 3:19-23 the Kingdom was still offered to Israel if they would repent.

(4) He told the parable of a Fig-Tree some months later, in Luke 13:5-9:

"I tell you, no; but unless you repent you will all likewise perish."
He also spoke this parable:
"A certain man (JESUS) **had a Fig Tree** (ISRAEL)
planted in his vineyard (the LAND),
and he came seeking fruit (FAITH) **on it and found none.**
Then he said to the Keeper of his Vineyard (the FATHER),
'Look, for three years (the ministry of Jesus)
I have come seeking fruit on this Fig Tree and find none.
Cut it down; why does it use up (waste) **the ground?'**
(notice that the cutting off of Israel will result in her removal from the land).
"But He answered and said to him, 'Sir, let it alone this year also,
until I dig around it and fertilise it.   And if it bears fruit, well.
But if not, after that you can cut it down.'"

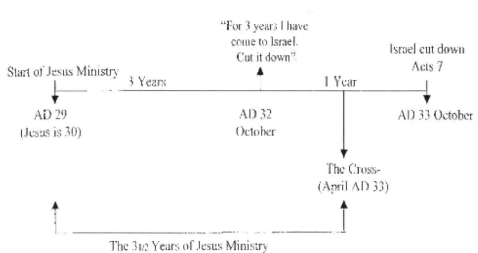

"For 3 years I have
come to Israel.
Cut it down"

Israel cut down
Acts 7

Start of Jesus Ministry

3 Years

1 Year

AD 29
(Jesus is 30)

AD 32
October

AD 33 October

The Cross-
(April AD 33)

The 3½ Years of Jesus Ministry

In this parable Jesus is warning Israel of coming destruction. Jesus is the man Who ministered for three years to Israel (the Fig-Tree) which was planted in the land (the Vineyard). He came looking for faith and found none and so at this stage He asked the Keeper (God, the Father) to cut the tree down because it was using up the ground but not fulfilling its purpose. The Keeper then requested that it have one more year of grace before judgement falls. If it responds - then good. If not - then after that year, Jesus will cut Israel off, which would result in her being expelled from the land. Now Jesus ministry was three and a half years, so this happened six months before the Cross. The extra year then ended six months after the Cross. Therefore when Israel did not repent, **Israel must have been officially cut off spiritually by Jesus six months after the Cross** for not bearing the fruit of faith. In turn this resulted in her destruction and removal from the land by the Romans in AD 70, as Jesus had predicted on many occasions.

This cutting off of Israel in AD 33, six months after the Cross, was such an important event that it must have been clearly marked in Scripture. Indeed, it is recorded in Acts 7 with Stephen's speech and martyrdom.

52

Although they were not yet cut off, Israel's clear rejection of Christ meant that at this stage of His ministry, Jesus no longer proclaimed the Kingdom as near and at hand but instead (as we shall see) He announced a delayed Kingdom and coming judgment (instead of glory) upon Israel for rejecting Him.

5. The Postponement of the Kingdom is pictured in Parables.

Luke and Matthew tell two similar parables about a Banquet for Israel.
Israel rejects the invitation, and as a result the invitation is given to a new group of people. However these parables are not identical and each teaches a distinctive truth. In Matthew's Parable, it is a Wedding-Banquet which symbolises the Messianic Kingdom (which includes the blessings of the New-Covenant). When Israel rejected the offer, the Banquet (Messianic Kingdom) was postponed and in the meantime she is judged and the invitation goes out to the whole world to become part of the future Messianic Kingdom.
In Luke's Parable the Banquet is not a Wedding, but represents participation in the blessings of the New-Covenant. When Israel rejected the invitation, the Banquet still takes place, but a whole new group (the Gentiles) are invited to partake of the New-Covenant in Christ (signifying the Church-Age).

Matthew 22:2-10 describes a Wedding-Banquet: **"The Kingdom of heaven is like a certain King** (God) **who arranged a Marriage Feast for His Son** (Jesus Christ), **and sent out His servants to call those who were invited to the Wedding** (Israel) **and they were not willing to come."**

The Marriage is between Christ and His Bride (all resurrected believers) which will happen at the opening of the Messianic Kingdom. The Millennium will start with the Marriage-Feast of the Lamb, and the whole Age is represented by a Feast, for the eating and drinking represents the receiving of all the New-Covenant blessings paid for by the Blood of Christ and freely poured out through the Holy-Spirit. Those who are invited to join the celebration are those still in their natural bodies. They are called to come and receive (feast on) the spiritual blessings of the New-Covenant, even though they are not resurrected yet. The first guests to be invited were Israel, for through the Abrahamic Covenant they were to have first place in the Kingdom. They had been previously invited through the prophets and were simply awaiting the time of Messiah's arrival, when they were to come to the Feast. At this time, God sent His servants (John the Baptist, Jesus and His disciples) to Israel, to call them to the Wedding-Feast. They preached: "The Kingdom is at hand, the time is now, Christ has come. Get ready, and come in faith to Christ."

But although they had been invited and called through the Gospel, they were not willing. The Kingdom (Feast) was offered to Israel, but the invitation was rejected.

"**Again, he sent out other servants, saying, 'Tell those who are invited, "See, I have prepared my dinner; my oxen and fatted cattle are killed, and all things are ready. Come to the Wedding."**
In the months after the sacrifice of Jesus Christ on the Cross, God again sent forth His servants (the apostles) to Israel to invite them to the Wedding (offering them the Messianic-Kingdom). Through His death, resurrection and outpouring of the Holy-Spirit at Pentecost, all things (all the provisions of the New-Covenant) were paid for, made ready and were on the table. Israel could still have believed in Christ and accepted the invitation and the Marriage-Feast (the Kingdom) would have been established then, but Israel rejected His offer of a King and a Kingdom: **"But they made light of it and went their ways, one to his own farm, another to his business. And the rest seized his servants, treated them spitefully, and killed them** (Israel's rejection of the Son was confirmed by the persecution of His servants). **But when the King heard about it, He was furious. And he sent out His armies, destroyed those murderers, and burned up their city** (as a judgement upon Israel's rejection of her Messiah, the Romans destroyed Jerusalem in AD 70). **Then He said to His servants: 'The Wedding (Kingdom) is ready, but those who were invited were not worthy** (God had been ready to establish the Kingdom, but because Israel rejected the offer, He had to delay the Wedding and the Feast). **Therefore go into the highways, and as many as you find, invite to the Wedding."** So

as a result of Israel's rejection of the invitation, the Feast (kingdom) is delayed for a time during which God starts a new programme of inviting all people to participate in the Feast (Kingdom), especially those who had previously been on the outside (the Gentiles). "**So those servants went out into the highways and gathered together all whom they found, both bad and good**" (In the Church Age, His servants go out into all the world to preach the Gospel to all people inviting them to be in God's Kingdom).

"**And** (as a result) **the Wedding Hall was filled with guests.**"
This shows the picture at the end of the age, when Jesus returns with the Wedding-Feast (the Messianic Kingdom) about to begin (v11). There are many who have accepted the invitation (the believers) and thus will become part of the Kingdom (Feast). Salvation is by grace, through believing and accepting God's invitation through the Gospel. At His Return Jesus will judge these believers according to their works, and they will be rewarded accordingly, or suffer loss of glory and opportunity (v11-14).

Luke 14:15-24 describes a Feast, but not necessarily a Wedding-Feast,
since the focus is now on feasting on the spiritual-blessings of the New-Covenant. Although these were originally associated with the Messianic-Kingdom; when Israel rejected this Kingdom, God gave these blessings to the Church (all those who accept the Gospel invitation to come and partake of this salvation): "**When one of those who were reclining at the table with Him heard this, He said to Him, "Blessed is everyone who will eat bread in the** (Messianic) **Kingdom of God!**"   **But He said to him, "A man was giving a big Dinner** (Feast), **and he invited many; and at the Dinner hour he sent his slave to say to those who had been invited, 'Come; for everything is ready now.'**

As in the Matthew Parable, Israel is invited to a Feast (to partake of the blessings of the New-Covenant, made ready through the Blood of Christ).
But they all alike began to make excuses (the feeble-ness of these excuses

revealed their unwillingness to come). **The first one said to him, 'I have bought a piece of land and I need to go out and look at it; please consider me excused.' Another one said, 'I have bought five yoke of oxen, and I am going to try them out; please consider me excused.' Another one said, 'I have married a wife, and for that reason I cannot come.' And the slave came back and reported this to his Master."** Most of Israel rejected Christ's gracious invitation to dine at His table.

"Then the head of the household became angry and said to his slave, 'Go out at once into the streets and lanes of the city and bring in here the poor and crippled and blind and lame.' And the slave said, 'Master, what you commanded has been done, and still there is room.' And the Master said to the slave, 'Go out into the highways and along the hedges and compel (urge) **them to come in, so that my house may be filled. 'For I tell you, none of those men who were invited shall taste of my dinner."**

The food (the New-Covenant blessings) would not be wasted and the Dinner would go ahead, but with a different group of guests. The invitation now goes out to all people (especially those who had not previously been invited - the Gentiles) to come and and share in the Feast of the spiritual blessings of the Kingdom through the New Covenant, while those for whom the Dinner was prepared and who had rejected the invitation are excluded from salvation (unbelieving Israel). Salvation is by grace, through believing and accepting Christ's invitation to come and feast at His table, receiving through faith His spiritual blessings, freely given to us in Christ.

6. The Church Announced. As Israel's rejection of Jesus gathered

strength, He announced the future building of His new assembly - the Church, distinct from Israel, which would be God's witness on earth for the time that Israel would be out of fellowship: **"On this Rock** (Jesus Christ) **I will build My Church, and the gates of Hades shall not prevail against it"** (Matthew 16:18) This is the first mention of the Church, which did not yet exist. Here Jesus explained who would be in the Church, and how the Church would be built (v13-17). The Church is built upon the foundation of Jesus and would be composed of those who have a personal revelation that He is the Christ, the Son of the Living God; those who believe in Him, confessing Him as Lord. Such a person would become a living stone ('petros' = Peter) built upon the Rock (the resurrected Christ) and thus he shares the nature of Christ and His victory over death and Hell. Jesus would build His Church through His death and resurrection: **"From that time Jesus began to show to His disciples that He must go to Jerusalem, suffer many things from the elders, chief priests and scribes, and be killed, and be raised the third day"** (v21).

As the time approached for His rejection by Israel to reach the inevitable climax of His death, He began to prepare his disciples for the coming events.

7. The Transfiguration However, Jesus still planned to establish

His Kingdom and to prove, thus He gave His disciples a picture-vision of His future Coming in Glory to establish His Kingdom - through the Transfiguration: **"The Son of Man will come in the glory of His Father with His angels, and then He will reward each according to his works. Assuredly, I say to you, there are some standing here who shall not taste death till they <u>see the Son of Man coming in His Kingdom</u>. Now after 6 days** (after 6,000 years will the Kingdom be established) **Jesus took Peter, James, and John up a high mountain by themselves and He was transfigured before them. His face shone like the sun, and His clothes became as white as the light. And behold, Moses and Elijah appeared to them, talking with Him. Peter said to Jesus, "Lord, it is good for us to be here; if You wish, I will make 3 tabernacles here, one for You, one for Moses, and one for Elijah." While He was speaking, a bright cloud over-shadowed them, and behold, a voice out of the cloud said, "This is My beloved Son, with whom I am well-pleased; listen to Him!"** (Matthew 16:28 -17:13).

<u>Peter's later comments confirm that the Transfiguration was a Type of the Coming Messianic Kingdom</u> (2 Peter1:16-19):

57

"**We did not follow cunningly devised fables when we made known to you the Power and Coming of our Lord Jesus Christ, but were eye witnesses of His Majesty.** For He received from God the Father, honour and glory when such a voice came to Him from the Excellent Glory:
"**This is My beloved Son, in whom I am well pleased."** And we heard this voice which came from heaven when we were with Him on the holy mountain.** And so we have the prophetic Word** (of His Coming and His Kingdom - through the Old Testament prophets) **confirmed** (by the sign of the Transfiguration - through the personal testimony of the New-Testament apostles), **which you do well to heed as a light that shines in a dark place** (it is still night in the world and so we have to live by the light of the world)**, until (1) the DAY** (the 1000-year Messianic Kingdom) **dawns** (when Christ will appear in glory, shining like the sun, for the Kingdom will be established by the Coming of Jesus Christ), **AND (2) the morning star rises in your hearts."**

Shortly before the sun rises to awaken the whole world, there is the appearance of the morning-star while it is still night (only seen by those who are awake). This speaks of a release (manifestation) of glory within the hearts of believers before the manifestation of the glory of the Son to the world. This is of course referring to the Rapture! Thus we have two prophesied manifestations of God to look forward to (the Rapture and Second-Coming of Christ). Until then we have the sure light of the Word of God to live by (consisting of the Old-Testament prophets, confirmed by the testimony of the New-Testament apostles (such as Peter). Notice that Peter said that the New-Testament confirmed the prophecies of the Old-Testament (rather than denying or reinterpreting them).

The main elements of the Kingdom were present in the Transfiguration.
1. A glorified Christ who reigns with the pleasure of the Father.
(These words of the Father confirmed Him in His Kingly Office, whereas at His baptism the Father confirmed Him in His prophetic office, and in John 12:28 the Father spoke again confirming Him in the High-Priestly ministry He was about to accomplish through His death and resurrection and ascension).

2. Glorified saints (Moses - typifying those who left the earth by death, and Elijah - typifying those who receive translation through the Rapture).

3. Believing Jews still alive on earth and enjoying the glory as represented by the three disciples.

8. As things stood with Israel, it was no longer possible for the Messianic Kingdom to come immediately.

On His final journey to Jerusalem, Jesus told a parable to prepare His disciples for the fact that He would be absent for a time and that the Kingdom would not be established immediately, since from prophecy and from his own preaching they would have assumed that He as the Messiah would establish the Kingdom right then.

Luke 19:11-27: **"Jesus told a parable, because He was near Jerusalem, and they supposed that the Kingdom of God was going to appear immediately. He said, "A nobleman** (Jesus) **went to a distant country** (the right hand of the Father) **to receive a Kingdom for himself, and then return"** (because the people rejected His right to rule, He had to go to a higher authority).

Something similar happened in Jesus' time. When Herod the Great died, Judea was left to his son Archelaus but that met with Jewish resistance. So he was delayed in becoming King and instead had to go away to Rome to receive authority to reign. The Jews sent a delegation of 50 men to Rome to tell Augustus that they did not want him as King. Rome agreed to let him rule and he eventually returned to rule with Rome's support.

Likewise Jesus is saying that He had to go away because Israel had rejected Him as King but He will return at the time set by the Father and with the Father's authority and the Kingdom will be established but there will be a lengthy delay. **"So he called ten of his servants, delivered to them ten minas, and said to them, 'Do business till I come'** (while He is absent, important work will be done - the Church Age). **But his citizens** (Israel) **hated him, and sent a**

59

delegation after him, saying, 'We will not have this man to reign over us'
(they continued their rejection of Him even after He ascended into Heaven).
**And so it was that when he returned, having received the Kingdom,
he then commanded these servants, to whom he had given the money,
to be called to him, that he might know how much every man had gained
by trading.** (When Jesus returns, He will establish the Kingdom,
but first He will judge and reward His servants - v16-26).

When He returns, He will also come with power and judge (kill) all those who
reject Him as King. **'But bring here those enemies of mine, who did
not want me to reign over them, and slay them before me'** (v27).
When He returns, only believers will be allowed to enter the Kingdom.

9. The last few days in Jerusalem.

Matthew 21: Jesus formally presented Himself as King in His Triumphal Entry in
fulfilment of Zechariah 9:9. **"This took place to fulfil what was spoken
through the prophet: 'SAY TO THE DAUGHTER OF ZION, 'BEHOLD YOUR
KING IS COMING TO YOU, GENTLE, AND MOUNTED ON A DONKEY,
EVEN ON A COLT, THE FOAL OF A BEAST OF BURDEN"** (v4,5).
Many welcomed Him with the official greeting to be given to Messiah:
**"The crowds going ahead of Him, and those who followed, were shouting,
"Hosanna to the Son of David; BLESSED IS HE WHO
COMES IN THE NAME OF THE LORD; Hosanna in the highest!"** (v9).

Luke 19:41-44: **"Now as He drew near, He saw the city and wept over it,
saying, "If you had known, _even you_, _especially in this your day, the
things that make for your peace!_ But now they are hidden from your
eyes. For days will come upon you when your enemies** (Rome) **will build
an embankment around you, surround you and close you in on every side,
and level you, and your children within you, to the ground;
and they will not leave in you one stone upon another, because
you did not know the time of your visitation."**

This was a special day when Israel should have officially accepted Christ and thereby ensure they would enter the Kingdom of peace. But their spiritual blindness concerning Him meant judgment for them, fulfilled by the Romans in AD 70. Again the reason for Jerusalem's destruction is that they did not recognise that they were living in the time of Messiah's visitation to Israel and thus rejected Him. As we shall see, they should have known from the prophet Daniel that they were living in such a time. His presentation included cleansing the Temple (v12,13) and healing the sick (v14) but the leaders opposed Him (v15); yet He confirmed his claims by receiving the praise of the people (v15,16).

The next day, following the leaders official rejection, He cursed a Fig-Tree. Matthew 21:18-22: "**Now in the morning, as He returned to the city, He was hungry. Seeing a Fig Tree by the road, He came to it and found nothing on it but leaves, and said to it, "Let no fruit grow on you ever again."** **Immediately the Fig Tree withered away. And when the disciples saw it** (the next day), **they marvelled, saying, "How did the Fig Tree wither away so soon?"** It immediately started to wither from the roots upwards, and by the next day the whole Tree was visibly withered (Mark 11:20). As before, the Fig-Tree represents Israel. Jesus had come to it but found no fruit (faith), only leaves (religion). Thus Jesus symbolically acted out on the Fig-Tree the judgement that would soon come upon Israel.

Israel had a call from God to bear fruit that the nations could eat. That is, she was to believe in God and His Messiah and communicate that faith to the world. She was specially anointed by God to be blessed and to be a blessing (Genesis 12:2). But even after the grace of Messiah had been poured out upon her, she was in unbelief (fruitless). This curse on Israel of her continually not bearing fruit signified that God was giving Israel over to her unbelief (her blindness and hardness of heart) for an extended period of time. Jesus also said: **"no man shall eat fruit from you again"** (Mark 11:14). This indicates that He was withdrawing her anointing to be God's witness to the nations. He judged the Fig-Tree (with fruitlessness) by cutting it off from its water supply (causing it to wither from the roots).   Likewise, later in AD 33, Jesus spoke the word to cut Israel off spiritually, resulting in her settled state of unbelief concerning Himself. As the judgement on the Tree was manifested the next day, so the cutting off of Israel was manifested physically later in AD 70, when Jerusalem was destroyed and Israel was dispersed to the nations.   This picture shows how Israel's cutting off resulted in her fruitlessness - her spiritual blindness and hardening of heart concerning her Messiah in this Age (Romans 11:25, 2Corinthians 3:14-16).

The conflicts with the leaders continued (Matthew 21:23-32) followed by a parable showing their attitude to Him. Matthew 21:33-46 also in Luke 20:9-19:

"There was a certain landowner (God) **who planted a vineyard** (believing Israel) **and set a hedge around it, dug a wine press in it and built a tower. And he leased it to vine dressers** (leaders) **and went into a far country** (Luke says also: 'for a long time') **Now when vintage-time drew near, he sent his servants to the vine dressers, that they might receive its fruit. And the vine dressers took his servants** (the prophets), **beat one, killed one, and stoned another.   Again he sent other servants, more than the first, and they did likewise to them.**

Then last of all he sent his Son (Jesus) **to them, saying, 'They will respect my beloved Son.'   But when the vine dressers saw the Son, they said among themselves, 'This is the heir.   Come, let us kill him and seize his inheritance.'   So they took him and cast him out of the vineyard and killed him.** (Here Jesus predicts that the Jewish leaders will kill Him).

Therefore, when the owner of the vineyard comes, what will he do to those vine dressers?"   They said to Him, "He will come and destroy those vine dressers (judgement came upon Israel in AD 70) **and give the Vineyard to others who will render to him the fruits in their seasons"**

"Jesus said to them, "Have you never read in the Scriptures: 'The stone (Jesus) **which the builders** (Israel's leaders) **rejected has become the chief Corner** (Pinnacle) **Stone.   This was the LORD'S doing,**

and it is marvellous in our eyes'?" The rejected and resurrected Christ will become the foundation of both the Church (Matthew 16:18) and the Messianic Kingdom (Daniel 2:34,35,44). **"Therefore I say to you, <u>the Kingdom of God will be taken from you and given to a nation bearing the fruits of it."</u>**

This has a double application. Firstly, the spiritual Kingdom of God during the Church Age has been taken from Israel and given to the (mostly Gentile) Church, so that the religious leaders of Israel are not God's representatives. Secondly, the Messianic Kingdom was taken from that generation of Israel, to be given to a later generation of Israel who will believe in Christ (bearing fruit).

"And whoever falls on this stone (rejects Christ) **will be broken; but on whoever it falls, it will grind him to powder** (judgement will fall upon those who reject Christ). **Now when the Chief Priests and Pharisees heard His parables, they perceived that He was speaking against them. And that very hour <u>they sought to lay hands on Him</u>** (to arrest Him), **but they feared the multitudes, because they took Him for a prophet."**

<u>In Matthew 23:</u> Jesus announces woes (judgements) upon Israel and her leaders because of their rejection of Him. E.g: **"Woe to you, scribes and Pharisees, hypocrites! For you shut up the Kingdom of heaven against men; for you neither go in yourselves, nor do you allow those who are entering to go in"** (v13). They, along with their fathers, were guilty of murdering the prophets and judgement would fall on that generation because they would reject and kill Messiah himself (v31-36).   **"Assuredly, I say to you, <u>all these things will come upon this generation</u>. O Jerusalem, Jerusalem, the one who kills the prophets and stones those who are sent to her! How often I wanted to gather your children together, as a hen gathers her chicks under her wings but <u>you were not willing!</u>"** (they rejected Him) **"See! <u>Your house is left to you desolate"</u>** (the Temple and Jerusalem was destroyed in AD 70) **"for I say to you, you shall see Me no more till you say, 'Blessed is He who comes in the name of the LORD!'"**
(Jesus will return when the nation and her leaders will receive Him, v37-39).

Having said this: **"Jesus went out and departed from the Temple"** (a prophetic action - the glory of God was leaving the Temple through the East Gate because of Israel's sin) **"and His disciples came up to show Him the buildings of the temple. Jesus said to them, "Do you not see all these things? Assuredly, I say to you, not one stone shall be left here upon another, that shall not be thrown down"** (now God had left the Temple, judgement would fall, and it did in AD 70- it was totally destroyed (Matt 24:1,2)

In His prophecy in Matthew 24 and Luke 21, Jesus again makes clear that the Kingdom will not come immediately but that Israel was to expect judgements instead, including the destruction of the Temple and the domination of Jerusalem by Gentiles and the dispersion to the nations (also Luke 23:27-31)

This was fulfilled in AD 66-73: **"When you see Jerusalem surrounded by armies, then know that its desolation is near. Then let those in Judea flee to the mountains, let those who are in the midst of her depart, and let not those who are in the country enter her. For these are the days of vengeance, that all things which are written may be fulfilled. But woe to those who are pregnant and to those who are nursing babies in those days! For there will be great distress in the land and wrath upon this people. And they will fall by the edge of the sword, and be led away captive into all nations. And Jerusalem will be trampled by Gentiles until the times of the Gentiles are fulfilled"** (Luke 21:20-24).

The Restoration of Israel. Luke 21:24: **"They will fall by the edge of the sword, and be led away captive into all nations. And Jerusalem will be trampled by Gentiles until the times of the Gentiles are fulfilled."** Even in predicting judgement, Jesus teaches that Israel will be restored to the land and to Jerusalem when the Times of the Gentiles were finished. Jesus also prophesied the restoration of Israel to the land in the parable of the Fig-Tree which we have seen represents Israel. The same Fig-Tree that we saw Him cut down and remove from the vineyard in Luke 13 and the same Fig-Tree that He cursed in Mark 11 will arise again and will be the great sign that we

64

are in the last generation before His return.   **"Look at the Fig Tree,
and all the Trees** (signs).   **When they are already budding, you see and
know for yourselves that Summer is now near.   So you also, when you see
these things happening, know that the Kingdom of God is near.   Surely, I
say to you, this generation** (that sees the Fig-Tree) **will
by no means pass away till all things take place"** (Luke 21:29-32).
Thus the Fig-Tree will reappear (Israel was reborn in 1948)   It talks of leaves
only, not fruit.   Other prophecy also shows Israel will first be regathered in
unbelief and then be converted.   This is a sign that the Messianic Kingdom
(Summer) brought in by Christ's return is near.   Jesus makes it clear that the
Messianic Kingdom is Coming - it is only delayed. He will fulfil what the prophets
said by Coming in Glory to establish the Kingdom (Matthew 24:29-31, 25:31-34).

In John chapters 14-17, Jesus prepared his disciples for the new dispensation
with teaching on the operation of the New Covenant in the Church Age and the
formation of the New Testament scriptures (John 14:26; 16:13,14).

10. The story of Israel's Rejection of Christ is continued in Acts.

ACTS 1: Acts 1:3 says that in the 40 days after His resurrection, Jesus spoke to
His disciples about the Kingdom of God.   Thus the developing Kingdom
Programme was the central issue to Jesus. So the disciples were well instructed
and when they asked Jesus: **"Will you at this time restore the Kingdom
to Israel?"** (Acts 1:6), it was a good question.   It is clear that they were still
expecting the Messianic Age, the Kingdom of God on earth spoken by the
prophets and promised to Israel (as the chief and holy nation). The issue was
not whether there would be such a Kingdom but when. Jesus didn't say He
would never do it, but: **"it is not for you to know the times or seasons that
the Father has fixed"** (v7). Jesus had never said it won't happen; He had just
indicated its possible delay because of Israel's attitude. So it will happen in God's
time! (The Kingdom was postponed because Israel rejected her Messiah, but
Jesus did not squash their Jewish expectation. Their hope for a literal Kingdom
was deliberately left intact by Jesus).   Israel still had six months to repent so a

definite answer was not possible. The Father however knew all things and had established set times and seasons to fulfil His plan for Israel. The Kingdom, though delayed, will be restored to Israel. The fulfilment of Gods plan and the Second Coming are directly linked with the return of Israel to the land.

Then Jesus revealed the purpose of the present age before this earthly Kingdom comes: **"But you shall receive power when the Spirit comes upon you and you shall be my witnesses to the ends of the earth"** (v8).
So, we are not looking to take over the world but to spread the Gospel.
We are looking to Jesus to return as King of Kings; only then will the Millennial Kingdom be established. Christian involvement in politics and society is good, for the purpose of holding back evil to help the Gospel go forth (1Timothy 2:1-4). Our destiny is to be on earth - to rule and reign with Christ here (Revelation 20, 1 Cor 6:2,3; Matthew 19:28, Luke 22:28-30). We are in training for reigning.

Acts 1:6,7 also shows that the Kingdom prophecies are not fulfilled by the Church, as Amillennialists hold, for then Jesus would have told them that the Kingdom was at that time being restored to Israel through the Church (spiritual Israel). But He put it off to an unknown future time. In whatever way you interpret Jesus' words, they do not fit with Amillennialists theology. For if Jesus understood the restoration of the Kingdom in a literal sense, then according to an Amillennialists, He should have said 'never' instead of encouraging them in a false hope. If He interpreted it spiritually (as fulfilled in the Church), He would have said 'that time is now, as you go and preach My Word.' But He implied a future fulfilment which could only be literal.

In ACTS 2 and 3, we see the preaching of the apostles to Israel.
They had now been given the final Sign of Jonah (Christ's resurrection after 3 days), and the outpoured Holy Spirit - if they rejected this final witness of the Spirit the nation would rejecting Christ (the unforgivable sin) and be cut off.

What really happened on the Day of Pentecost (Acts 2)?
To interpret what God was doing, Peter (in v17-21) quoted Joel 2:28-32 (a

prophecy of the outpouring of the Spirit and great signs and wonders in the time leading up to the Coming of the Messiah to establish the Messianic-Kingdom) saying: **"this is that which was spoken by the prophet Joel."** However the events of that day clearly did not bring a complete fulfillment of Joel's prophecy. By saying **'this is that'** Peter was indicating that what was happening on that day was just a foretaste of what Joel had talked about. This problem can be solved if one recognises that the Kingdom was still being offered to Israel. This was God's time to bring the nation of Israel into the New-Covenant (mediated by Christ, the prophet like unto Moses) on the anniversary of the Old Covenant at Sinai (mediated by Moses). But first, Israel had to receive Christ and His New-Covenant salvation by believing in Him and calling upon His Name (Joel 2:32). (The Holy-Spirit was poured out and there to help them repent and turn to Christ). Thus Peter called Israel to repent (of their rejection of Christ) so that they could receive the Holy Spirit (Acts 2:38,39). If Israel had received Christ, she would have entered the New Covenant as a nation and possessed the Kingdom that same year. But the leaders rejected Him and the prophecy was unfulfilled. God, however still gave the Spirit to the remnant of Israel who believed. So Peter rightly saw the day of Pentecost as the first stage in the fulfilment of Joel's prophecy, that the Kingdom was being offered and that the outpouring of the Spirit was confirmation that God was ready to establish the Kingdom. However the complete fulfilment of Joel's prophecy is delayed until the Second Coming because of Jewish unbelief.

In Acts 3:19-21, Peter told Israel that the offer was still on the table for that generation if they repented of their rejection of Christ. He said to Israel: **"Repent and be converted, that (1) your sins may be blotted out, so that Times** ('Kairos') **of Refreshing may come from the Presence of the Lord,** (these are spiritual blessings of the New-Covenant, originally meant for Israel to prepare her for life in the Messianic-Kingdom that was about to begin, but when the nation rejected the Messiah, this offer was still made to all individuals in the Church-Age) **and that (2) He may send Jesus Christ, who was preached to you before, whom Heaven must receive**

until the Times ('Chronos' = Age) **of the Restoration of all things,**
which God has spoken by the mouth of all His holy prophets
since the world began." The 'Times of the Restoration of all things' is the
Messianic Kingdom, as predicted by all the prophets, in which Christ will restore
the earth to its original state before the Fall, with satan and the curse removed,
and Christ personally reigning as King from Jerusalem (a perfect Theocracy) and
outpoured spiritual blessings - 'the Times of Refreshing'.

This Kingdom can only be established on earth by Christ Himself when He
returns from Heaven. Here Peter promises that Jesus will indeed return to
establish the Kingdom in fulfilment of all the prophets, but that He will only do this
in response to the national repentance of Israel. If they had repented at that
time, Jesus would have returned that year, but their rejection of Christ continued.
Peter goes on to say that Jesus is the promised 'Prophet like unto Moses' (Deut
18:15-19) whom they must obey (the Messiah). Like Moses, He has mediated a
New Covenant and will lead them into the Promised Land (the Kingdom-Age)
if they follow Him (v22). The prophecy says that if they reject Him, they shall be
utterly destroyed (v23). Peter is warning them about what will happen if they
reject Christ. God sent Him in fulfilment of all the prophets to first of all deal with
sin, and if they will receive this New Covenant ministry He would also set up the
Messianic Kingdom through Israel (v19-26).

ACTS 4 shows the leaders continuing in their opposition.

ACTS 7 - STEPHEN'S SPEECH Six months after the Cross, time has run out
and Israel are cut off by God at Stephen's speech (see the parable in Luke 13).
Had they received 'the prophet like Moses', they would have entered
the New Covenant and possessed the Kingdom. Israel's leaders now had
the Sign of Jonah and had rejected the Holy Spirit (Jesus had warned them
of this in Matthew 12). They had every proof and every chance to repent.
Their sin was a repeat of the sins of their fathers (only intensified)
and so will be the consequences.

Stephen's whole speech is exactly what you would expect at a judicial cutting off of Israel - a clear expose of Israel's sin and revelation of the consequent judgement.

His Conclusion is 7:51-53 (c.f. Matthew 23:32-39):
"You stiff necked and uncircumcised in heart and ears!
You always resist the Holy Spirit; as your fathers did, so do you.
Which of the prophets did your fathers not persecute?
And they killed those who foretold the coming of the Just One,
of whom you now have become the betrayers and murderers,
who have received the law by the direction of angels and have not kept it.
As your fathers did, so do you."

So Stephen reveals Israel's sin throughout history as illustrations of their own sin (done in a subtle way - showing due respect for the fathers).
In that generation, Israel's sin had come to fullness and so was ripe for judgement.   So Stephen's speech to Israel is all about their UNBELIEF (their unrepentant rejection of Christ).   They confirmed that they were hardened in this rejection by murdering Stephen - the first Christian martyr, just as they had killed Jesus.   And so God finally cut them off.   Stephen also predicts the postponement of the Kingdom as the consequence of their sin.

He gives examples of Israel's SIN and it's CONSEQUENCE (the postponement of the Kingdom).   These are foreshadowings of what is going on in AD 33.
1. Abraham (Acts 7:2-5) - sin delayed him entering the land (Kingdom) He remained in Haran for maybe 40 years until his father died. So natural attachments and traditions caused his entrance into the land to be postponed.

2. The Twelve Patriarchs (v5-8).   Their sins resulted in bondage to a foreign power (Egypt).

3. Joseph (v9-16). A TYPE of CHRIST - 'killed' by his brothers (the first Coming of Christ). They did not know he was alive and exalted as lord but he revealed himself to his repentant brothers the second time (the Second Coming) and they then enter into blessing.   Seven lean years (the Tribulation) will eat up the seven fat years of Christ's ministry at his first Coming (AD 26-33).   Israel will come to her Joseph in the Tribulation and eat of the grain (truth) laid up from the first seven years (Jesus is the Christ). See later comments on Daniel 9:24-27 (the key prophecy of these cancelled seven years and the Kingdom-Postponed) for more explanation of this. It was sufficiently enigmatic that it could not be understood fully until the Kingdom offer was rejected and so did not prejudice the offer.   The Church age is in the gap between the two sets of seven years.

4. Moses (1) (v17-36). <u>A TYPE OF CHRIST</u> - v37.
As the prophet like unto Moses, Jesus would have brought them into the New Covenant (Pentecost) and into the Kingdom. Israel rejected Moses when he came to them the first time as their deliverer (v25). The result was a delay of 40 years with Moses absent.
5. Moses (2) (v38-43). When Moses led them out of Egypt, Israel rejected him and turned to idolatry.   Their unbelief meant that that generation did not enter the promised land
but was delayed in entering the land for 40 years.

6. David (v44-47) could not build the Temple - it was left to a future generation
because he was guilty of murder.   Solomon's Kingdom is a type of the Messianic Age where true worship will be established (symbolised by the Temple).

CONCLUSION: (v48-50).   Even Solomon's Temple worship was not the ultimate, but a type of the true worship that Christ would bring, where man would be the Temple of the Holy Spirit. This was the New Covenant blessing for the Kingdom (Ezekiel 36).
But in rejecting the SPIRIT, they were rejecting the Kingdom and it would be POSTPONED.

Putting these types together, we see Israel given a promise to POSSESS THE LAND
(the KINGDOM) but because of UNBELIEF, there is a POSTPONEMENT,
and the offer is made again to a later generation.
(1) Seven years of blessing (Joseph). But in which the King is rejected.
(2) 40 (Jubilee) years of delay in the wilderness of nations (Moses).
(3) Seven years of famine (Tribulation) (Joseph) In which the King is accepted.

So, Jesus Christ came offering the literal Kingdom to Israel. He died and rose again at the close of the 490th year of Daniel 9:24 (the Great Jubilee). Had they accepted Christ, He would have immediately established the Kingdom in AD 33 and Israel would have entered the New Covenant at PENTECOST. But instead Israel rejected Christ and so the promised Messianic Kingdom could not be established at that time. Israel was spiritually cut off later in October 33 (at the end of the Jubilee year), leading to her being removed from the land soon after (70). In place of the Messianic Kingdom God inserted the Mystery Kingdom (Church-Age) in which His Plan for the Gentiles could be manifested.   After this He will move to fulfil His plan for Israel.

Thus the transition from the Age of Israel to the Age of the Church was effected in AD 33.

At this point in Acts 7, the Church had begun but it was entirely Jewish. The official cutting off of Israel is the key moment, the turning point in Acts, the signal for the Gospel to go out to the rest of the world. **"At that time a great persecution arose against the Church which was at Jerusalem; and they were all scattered throughout the regions of Judea and Samaria, except the apostles"** (Acts 8:1). At this time the Church did not yet fully understand God's programme for the Gentiles in this Age (Acts 1:8), but now Israel was cut off, God began to supernaturally lead them into new territory with the Gospel and they began to see the Mystery come to pass. In Acts 8, the Gospel went to Samaria (half-Jews) and in Acts 10 it went to the Gentiles for the first time. God poured out the Spirit upon these ones as on the day of Pentecost without them having to become Jews by circumcision. In this way God signified that Israel had been cut off and He was doing a new thing in this Age, working through the Church (a New Man comprised of Jew and Gentile as equals) - not national Israel. Also in Acts 9, soon after Stephen's death and connected with it (7:58) is Paul's conversion, who is then called to be the apostle to the Gentiles and who was used by God to complete the revelation of the Mystery. Thus the Holy-Spirit led the apostles into all the (Church-Age) truth they were not ready to receive before (John 16:12,13).

In Acts 13:46-48, Paul says that Israel was given the first opportunity but because she rejected the Gospel, God was turning to the Gentiles.

This is confirmed in Acts 28:25-28: **"When they** (the Jews) **did not agree among themselves, they departed after Paul had said one word: "The Holy Spirit spoke rightly through Isaiah the prophet to our fathers, saying, 'Go to this people and say: "Hearing you will hear, and shall not understand; and seeing you will see, and not perceive; for the hearts of this people have grown dull. Their ears are hard of hearing, and their eyes they have closed, lest they should see with their eyes and hear with their ears, lest they should understand with their hearts and turn, so that I should heal them." Therefore let it be known to you that the salvation of God has been sent to the Gentiles, and they will hear it!"** Some (following Bullinger) understand this speech as marking the final cutting off of Israel, but passages in Luke 13, 2Corinthians 3 and Romans 11 show that Israel was cut off before this time (AD62). Paul is simply saying that Israel have already been cut off and are under a judicial blindness as Isaiah had prophesied.

The fact that Israel rejected her Messiah is no grounds for anti-semitism today. All of us - the Gentiles as well as Israel, were responsible for the crucifixion of Christ; for it was our sin that took Him to the Cross, and so this is no excuse for anti-semitism. It is just that Israel's rejection of her Christ is more significant as far as the Kingdom Programme is concerned.   In fact, it was only the generation of Jesus day that was guilty of rejecting Him when He came.   Moreover Israel's rejection opened the door for the salvation of many Gentiles which was part of God's purpose, so God worked it all for good (Romans 8:28).

11. <u>THE CUTTING OFF OF ISRAEL IN ROMANS 11</u>

Writing later (AD 57), Paul in the Book of Romans, speaks of Israel as having already been cut off, so that the Gentiles could come under God's favour and enter into the New Covenant.

<u>In Romans 9-11,</u> Paul explains the present situation of Israel.
1. God has made promises to her that He will keep (9:1-5).
2. These promises are made and will be fulfilled to believing Israel, called the remnant, who have both the genes and the faith of Abraham (v6,27-29). This is illustrated in God's choice of Isaac and Jacob to inherit the covenant (9:6-13).   This means Israel has a guaranteed future.
3. God is just to judge those who reject Him, even if they are of Israel, and He is able to show mercy to those who believe, even if they are Gentiles (9:14-26).
4. The majority of Israel rejected Christ and the New Covenant (9:30-10:21) and so God could not fulfil His promises to the nation at that time. Instead He turned to the Gentiles as He had warned He would (10:19,20).

<u>Romans 11:1,2:</u> **"I say then, has God cast away His people? Certainly not! For I also am an Israelite, of the seed of Abraham, of the tribe of Benjamin. God has not cast away His people whom He foreknew."**

God has not finished with Israel - the cutting off is not permanent.
Israel is part of God's Eternal Purpose, in which she has been sovereignly chosen by God, so she will stand. This is ensured by God's Sovereign Grace in always preserving a remnant of true believers (the Israel of God, see v2-6).
Even though the nation rejected Christ, and was judicially blinded (cut off), failing to obtain righteousness through the New Covenant (v7-10), yet there was a remnant that believed and obtained it (v7). The existence of this remnant confirms that God has not finished with Israel and that she has a future.

<u>v11,12:</u> **"I say then, have they stumbled that they should fall?**

Certainly not!   But through their fall (lit: trespass), **to provoke them to jealousy, salvation has come to the Gentiles. Now if their fall is riches for the world, and their failure riches for the Gentiles, how much more their fullness!"**   God is not finished with Israel. They have stumbled but have not fallen in such a way as not to rise again. While they are down, God has brought in the Church-Age for salvation to go to the Gentiles; but even this is part of God's purpose in bringing the salvation of Israel, which in turn will bring great blessing to the world through the Messianic Kingdom. Paul's motive in his ministry is to bring the Gentiles into such blessing that Israel will realise she has missed it and turn back to Christ (v13,14).

v15: **"For if their being cast away is the reconciling of the world, what will their acceptance be but life from the dead?"**   National Israel has been cut off, allowing salvation to go to the world, but she will repent, come to faith in Christ and be accepted again and this will allow the world to move into the Messianic Age, through the Return of Christ. He will restore and regenerate the earth (Matthew 19:28), resurrect all remaining dead believers and bring spiritual revival to the nations.   In every respect it will be 'life from the dead', not just for Israel. The blessing of the whole earth is tied up with Israel's faith.

v16: **"For if the first fruit is holy, the lump is also holy; and if the root is holy, so are the branches."**
Her origins in Abraham (and his unconditional Covenant with God) are holy and this ensures her destiny.   This 'root and branches' is the start of a picture of how God's favour and blessing flows to mankind - **THE OLIVE TREE**.

Those who have tried to get to grips with the detailed symbolism of the Olive Tree in verses 16-25 will appreciate the difficulties.   One important issue is knowing whether individuals or nations are being referred to. Another distinction that must be made is between temporary (unbelieving) branches and permanent, fruitful (believing) branches - both of which are seen in nature.

I aim to present an interpretation consistent with all the precise language used.

The root is the Abrahamic Covenant (Genesis 12:1-3). From the root flows the nourishing sap (fatness) to the branches (v17) - God's goodness, blessing and favour (v22). Those branches (people) who believe, draw upon the sap and produce good fruit (olives). Olive Oil was used for COMFORT, HEALING, ANOINTING and LIGHT, representing the ministry of the HOLY SPIRIT. The Olive Tree therefore represents God's chosen and anointed witnesses to the world. However not all the branches are believers (v20-22), so inclusion is not simply based on an individual's faith. In fact, inclusion firstly depends on national identity! (Of course, unbelieving fruitless branches will eventually be removed).

For 2000 years after Abraham the branches were those who were 'in Abraham', the seed of Abraham, the nation of Israel. They were 'the natural branches' because they were physically descended from Abraham, Isaac and Jacob. Being in the Olive Tree entitled them to partake of God's covenant blessings (goodness) and to be part of God's anointed witness (a light to the nations) so that the world would be blessed through Israel. So the Olive Tree was identified with Israel (Jeremiah 11:16; Hosea 14:6). However not all the branches believed and drew upon the blessing of God that was available to them and so were fruitless. Thus, being in the Tree was for all of Israel, but not all of these partook of the blessings of salvation. When Israel (as a nation) was cut off for unbelief, the Gentile nations were grafted in (v17,19,24). As with Israel this does not mean that all the branches are believers, but that God's favour has moved from Israel to the Gentile nations for the next 2000 years, for their salvation (v11). As history verifies, the anointing shifted to the Gentile nations for the proclamation of God's Word. However Paul warns the Gentiles that at the end of their time-period of grace that they (like Israel) will be cut off if they are in unbelief concerning Christ (v21,22). This in turn will lead to Israel being grafted back in again when she begins to turn from her unbelief (v23,24).

It is important to see that God's actions of 'cutting off' and 'grafting in' are actions upon national entities. Thus Paul is saying that Israel as a nation has a future with God (not just individual Jews). Those branches in the Olive Tree who receive the sap and bear fruit are the individual believers. When Israel was cut off in AD 33 it was for unbelief. It follows that the remnant (those who believed in Christ) were not cut off (see v7). This was possible because their position was secured by being in Christ (Abraham's Seed) rather than being of Israel.

That is why v17 says: "**and if <u>some of the branches</u> were broken off...**"
This verse proves that there was a CUTTING OFF of branches from the OLIVE TREE before Paul wrote Romans. Israel as a nation was cut off as God's anointed representative for rejecting Christ (this is Israel during the Church Age but not all Israel for all time). Believing Jews were put in Christ and received a great anointing (sap) at Pentecost. For the next few months they formed a purely Jewish Church. Then when Israel was cut off later that year (Acts 7) these were not cut off.

<u>On the very day Israel was cut off, God grafted in the Gentile nations</u>:
"**and you** (the Gentile nations) **being a wild Olive Tree,**
were grafted in among them (the remnant of Israel)" (v17b).

Thus the Gentiles came under God's special favour. Moreover, those Gentiles who believed in Christ could actually partake of the blessing of Abraham, the promise of the Holy Spirit: "**and with them** (the remnant of Israel) **became a partaker of the root and fatness of the Olive Tree**" (v17c) When a Gentile believes his position in the Olive Tree is secured because he is put into Christ (who is the physical Seed of Abraham) and given His righteousness (His standing in the Covenant) and thus becomes an inheritor of the promise:
"**<u>If you are Christ's, then you are Abraham's seed, and heirs according to the promise</u>**" (Galatians 3:29). "**He redeemed us that the blessing of Abraham might come upon the Gentiles <u>in Christ Jesus</u>, that we might receive the promise of the Spirit through faith**" (Galatians 3:14).
Thus believing Gentiles become the spiritual seed of Abraham and inherit the blessings of the New Covenant (see also Romans 4).

<u>Likewise when a Jew believes in Christ he is joined to the Olive Tree only by virtue of being in Christ</u>: "**But their minds were made dull** (Israel's cutting off and blindness happened before Paul wrote Corinthians) **for to this day**

the same veil remains when the old covenant is read.   It has not been removed (the nation is still cut off and blinded), **because only in Christ is it taken away. Even to this day when Moses is read, a veil covers their hearts. But whenever anyone turns to the Lord, the veil is taken away**" (2Corinthians 3:14-16, NIV). When a Jew believes, he is restored to the Tree and the New Covenant blessings but only because he is now in Christ (not because of his nationality).   In Christ, the veil (separation) is removed automatically, so that he can enjoy the fullness of the Spirit (v17,18). The end-result is that, at this time, believing Jews and Gentiles (forming the Church) have a position of complete equality in the Tree, because their position is only due to being in Christ. We still have a national identity but it is not a factor as far as our position in the Church is concerned.

Paul summarises this in Galatians 3:26-29: **"For you are all sons of God through faith in Christ Jesus. For as many of you as were baptised into Christ have put on Christ. There is neither Jew nor Greek, there is neither slave nor free, there is neither male nor female; for you are all one in Christ Jesus. And if you are Christ's, then you are Abraham's seed, and heirs according to the promise."**

In Summary, in AD33, the nation of Israel was cut off and the Gentile Nations were grafted into the Olive Tree. So there has been a special favour upon the Gentile nations. However many of the branches (individuals) were temporary branches (unbelievers). Anyone (Jew or Gentile) who believes in Christ is a new-creation in Christ and becomes a permanent fruit bearing branch (in the Church, in Christ, John 15). Thus the Church has been God's functioning witness.   God's grafting in and blessing of the Gentile nations however is not permanent. As God judged Israel, so He must also judges the Gentile nations, both for their unbelief and for their treatment of Israel:

v18-22:   A WARNING to the GENTILE NATIONS to beware of being in pride over Israel by saying that God has finished with them:
"Do not boast against the (natural) **branches** (Israel). **But if you do boast,**

**remember that you do not support the root, but the root supports you.
You will say then, 'Branches were broken off that I might be grafted in.'
Well, <u>because of unbelief they were broken off</u>, and you stand by faith. Do
not be haughty, but fear. For if God did not spare the natural branches
(Israel), He may not spare you** (Gentile nations) **either.
Therefore consider the goodness and severity of God: on those who fell,
severity; but toward you, goodness, if you continue in His goodness.
<u>Otherwise you also will be cut off</u>."** <u>He warns of a future CUTTING OFF of
the GENTILE NATIONS for their unbelief in Christ and their pride over Israel.</u>

This shows that the branches that were grafted in were not just the believing Gentiles, for God
would not cut off true believers. Therefore the branches grafted in at AD33 and who are in
danger of being cut off must be the Gentile nations generally. As Israel had to be cut off
before the Gentiles could be grafted in, so the Gentiles must be cut off before Israel can be
grafted in again. Therefore this must happen before the Tribulation, for after the Rapture of the
Church, Israel must become God's representatives again during the Tribulation (the last
7 years of Daniel's 490 years which were allocated to them before the Messianic Kingdom -
see Daniel 9:24-27). I believe this cutting off of the Gentiles has already happened in 1933
at the end of a Gentile grace-period of exactly 1960 (lunar) years = 1900 solar years = 40
Jubilees from AD33 (a full explanation will have to wait for a later book on Bible Chronology).
This event led to World-War 2 and the present build-up to the Tribulation, and finally for the
troubles and judgements upon the world in the Tribulation itself. It also allowed the rebirth of
ISRAEL and her restoration to the Land in 1948, and the recapture of Jerusalem in 1967,
which was the sign that the Times of the Gentiles (the Times of Gentile dominion of Israel
which began in about 600 BC with the Babylonian Captivity - see Part 3 for more on this)
had ended, according to Luke 21:24: "**Jerusalem shall be trodden down of the Gentiles,
until the times of the Gentiles be fulfilled.**" Jesus says plainly that when Israel is a free
nation and Jerusalem is back under permanent Jewish control, the times of the Gentiles will
then be fulfilled. This happened in June 1967, signalling that we are now in the final phase
of the Church Age! The period of spiritual favour to the Gentile nations (AD33-1933) was a
special period within the Times of the Gentiles. Israel being cut off spiritually and the Gentile
nations being grafted into God's favour (in AD 33) led to an increase of political Gentile
dominion over Israel, demonstrated by Jerusalem's destruction by the Gentiles and the
scattering of Israel to the nations in AD 70 (see Luke 21:20-24). The ending of the Times of
the Gentiles and the restoration of Israel's dominion as demonstarted by her rebirth (1948)
and sovereignty over Jerusalem (1967), indicates that the Gentiles must have been previously

cut off from her place of favour (1933).   As Israel's spiritual cutting off led to a further loss of dominion for Israel, so the Gentile cutting off led to a loss of Gentile political dominion over Israel.   As the Gentile ingrafting led to greater Gentile dominion over Israel, so her cutting off from favour (AD 1933) led to a decrease in Gentile dominion over Israel, which made possible the ending of the Times of the Gentiles in the rebirth of Israel and recapture of Jerusalem. Thus it was necessary that the Gentile nations were cut off according to Romans 11:22, before the Times of Gentile political dominion over Israel could be fulfilled (Luke 21:24). God's spiritual action in 1933 released rearrangements to take place through World War 2, that ultimately led to the manifestation in 1948-the miraculous rebirth of Israel as a free nation.

Thus these events in the last century confirm that the Gentiles have been cut off just as Paul warned would happen, and that therefore we are now in a special period of time just before the Tribulation. Both the Gentile nations and Israel are now cut off (only the Church is grafted in), and the world is quickly moving toward the conditions and final judgements of the Tribulation.   With Israel and the nations cut off, God is allowing the world to move towards its final condition in the Tribulation when it will be ripe for judgement. This includes moves towards a One-World Government, Economy and Religion. The growth of sin is also causing increasing the sorrows that Jesus described (Matthew 24:7), especially anti-Semitism (as shown in the Holocaust).   When the Church is raptured, the final restraint on evil will be removed and all these things will come to fullness in the Tribulation and then God will judge them. The Gentile nations have been cut off, but the true Church is of course still part of the Olive Tree as God's anointed witness. The Church is present now to bring in a final world-wide harvest of souls before the Tribulation begins.   After the Rapture, Jesus will SPEW OUT of His mouth the apostate anti-semitic Church that remains (Revelation 3:16) and graft Israel back in as His witness.

Next, Paul predicts that after the Gentile Nations are cut off, then ISRAEL (as a nation) will be GRAFTED back in: "**And they** (Israel) **also, if they do not continue in unbelief, will be grafted in, for God is able to graft them in again. For if you were cut out of the Olive Tree which is wild by nature, and were grafted contrary to nature into a cultivated olive tree, how much more will these, who are natural branches, be grafted into their own Olive**

Tree?" (v23-24). The cutting off of the Gentiles opens the way for Israel to be grafted back in, but this hasn't happened yet because of her unbelief.

The next verse (v25) tells us when it will happen: **"For I do not desire, brethren, that you should be ignorant of this mystery, lest you should be wise in your own opinion, that blindness in part** (it is not total or final) **has happened to Israel until the fullness of the Gentiles has come in."** Israel will be cut off (blinded) until the harvest of the Church-Age is complete - which is the moment of RAPTURE. After the dramatic sign of the Rapture (confirming the Messiahship of Jesus), there will be a turning to Christ in Israel and God will graft Israel in again as God's anointed witness for the Tribulation (with the Church removed God needs a witness in the earth). This is confirmed by the sealing of 144,00 evangelists from the 12 tribes of Israel at the start of the Tribulation (which is the last seven years of the Age of Israel according to Daniel 9:24-27). Thus in the Tribulation, Israel is grafted in but the Gentiles are not, which is as it was before the Cross. In fact, as we shall see, the 7-year Tribulation is a rerun of the 7-year Presentation of Messiah to Israel (AD26-33), because they rejected Him the first time. But this time, by the end of the Tribulation the nation as a whole receives Jesus as Lord.

During the Tribulation, with their blindness lifted, Israel will increasingly come to see and believe in Jesus and at the end of the Tribulation, the whole nation will receive Jesus as her Messiah - leading to the Return of Christ for their salvation (both physical and spiritual): **"And so all Israel will be saved, as it is written: "The Deliverer will come out of Zion, and He will turn away ungodliness from Jacob; for this is My Covenant with them, when I take away their sins"** (v26,27). He delivers them from their enemies at the Battle of Armageddon and saves them from their sins through bringing the whole nation into the New Covenant for the Messianic Kingdom. Thus, '**all Israel will be saved**' summarises the complete restoration of the nation of Israel in the Kingdom. This is proof positive that God has not finished with Israel but will fulfil all His promises and covenants to her in the Millennium.

Conclusion: "**Concerning the Gospel they are enemies for your sake, but concerning the election they are beloved for the sake of the fathers. For the gifts and the calling of God are without repentance**" (v28,29). God's choosing and calling of Israel will not be revoked (taken away). The stewardship of Jerusalem and the Promised Land is given to her for all time. This is not because she is faithful but because God is faithful to His covenants. He will still fulfil His Purpose and Promise for Israel.

"**For as you were once disobedient to God, yet have now obtained mercy through their disobedience, even so these also have now been disobedient, that through the mercy shown you, <u>they also may obtain mercy.</u> For God has shut up all to disobedience** (He cut Israel off for a time) **that He might have mercy on all**" (that full salvation might go to all the world - in the Church Age, v30-32). <u>God will reveal the true Messiah to Israel</u> and she will come back to God, even through the loving witness of the true Church. The issue of Jesus is for Jews a painful historical wound, with much persecution being done 'in His name'. Often the Church has been anti-semitic blaming the Jews for killing Jesus, forgetting that the Gentiles were part of it also, in fact it was all our sins that led Him to lay down His own life for us on the Cross. But Israel, with the help of the Spirit, will see that Jesus Himself was a righteous Jew who alone fulfilled all the requirements of Messiahship. The sins committed by some of His followers do not nullify His claims, any more than the sins of Israel do not nullify Abraham and Moses. Israel will discern the cause of her 2000-year dispersion, but that it has not been all bad. She will see that through Christ and the Gospel, the truth of the God of Israel has gone to all nations as never before (as the prophets predicted). They will see that God has even worked their disobedience for the salvation of Gentiles and they will praise God for His wonderful sovereign wisdom, just as Paul did (v33-36).

Although the Nation of Israel didn't enter into the New Covenant, the believing Remnant of Israel did. National Israel was not cut off for another four months (until then the Church was all Jewish) When Israel didn't repent, God initiated

His Mystery Plan.   God still brought the Remnant of Jewish believers into the New Covenant at Pentecost - and they became the CHURCH. They came into the possession of spiritual blessings that were originally associated with the Messianic Kingdom (Joel 2), being '**the powers of the Age to come**' (Hebrews 6:5).   God kept His appointment and anointed them to spread the Word to the nations. When Israel was cut off 4 months later in October at the end of the Jubilee Year (Acts 7), He was able to graft in the Gentiles and that is when Gentile believers in Christ started coming into the Church, with full equality with the Jewish believers (see Acts 8, Acts 10) which was a great shock to the Jews. When the Church Age is completed at the Rapture, the final seven years of Israel will run again (the Tribulation) and this time they will receive him as Messiah and the Messianic Kingdom will then be established (Romans 11:25-27)

THE ELIJAH PROPHECIES

This key of the Kingdom rejected and postponed enables us to understand the hard scriptures concerning John the Baptist and Elijah.

1. Elijah must come before the Messiah to prepare Israel.
"Behold, I send My messenger, and he will prepare the way before Me...Behold, I will send you Elijah the prophet before the coming of the great and dreadful day of the LORD. He will turn The hearts of the fathers to the children, and the hearts of the children to their fathers, lest I come and strike the land with a curse" (Malachi 3:1, 4:5,6).

2. But instead of Elijah, John was sent in his place. **"He** (John) **will also go before Him in the spirit and power of Elijah, 'to turn the hearts of the fathers to the children,' and the disobedient to the wisdom of the just, to make ready a people prepared for the Lord"** (Luke1:17). He had many similarities to Elijah in his dress and diet, his confrontational style of ministry, his being in the wilderness three and a half years calling Israel to repentance, preparing the way for a greater one to come (Elisha is a type of Christ).

3. John denied that he was Elijah.   The Jews expected Elijah to come first so they asked John if he was Elijah: **"What then? Are you Elijah?"**

He said, "I am not." "Are you the Prophet?" And he answered, "No."
Then they said to him, "Who are you, that we may give an answer
to those who sent us?   What do you say about yourself?"
He said: "I am 'The voice of one crying in the wilderness:
"Make straight the way of the LORD'" (John 1:21-23). So John did not
fulfil the Elijah prophecy - he was a prefigurement of the yet-to-come Elijah.

4. Jesus keeps John and Elijah distinct. "His disciples asked Him,
"Why then do the scribes say that Elijah must come first?"
And He answered and said, "Elijah is coming and will restore all things;
but I say to you that Elijah already came, and they did not recognise him,
but did to him whatever they wished. So also the Son of Man is going to
suffer at their hands."   Then the disciples understood that He spoke to
them about John the Baptist" (Matthew 17:10-13, Mark 9:11-13).
Jesus divides the prophesied ministry of Elijah into two persons and phases:
(1) Elijah will come in the future to prepare Israel for the Kingdom.
(2) Elijah has come in the person of John, but Israel rejected both John and
Jesus. So, although John is not Elijah, John fulfilled the ministry prophesied of
Elijah but Israel rejected it.

5. The Jews were right to say Elijah must come just before Messiah comes to
set up the Kingdom.   So why did John come instead of Elijah in AD 33?   God,
in His foreknowledge, knew that Israel would reject her Messiah and that His
Kingdom would be postponed. Then the prophecy of Elijah coming just before
the Great and Terrible Day of the Lord (judgment for all the earth before the
Kingdom) would not come to pass.   So God sent John in his place, with the
same spirit and power, to prepare the way.   Then after the Church Age, Elijah
himself will come and minister to Israel in the Tribulation (just before the Second
Advent of Christ - the Great and Terrible Day of the Lord) and successfully
prepare them for the Kingdom.   This is how we know one of the two witnesses
of Revelation 12 ministering in the Temple must be Elijah. Thus God will fulfil the
Elijah prophecy literally as well as providing first century Israel with every
opportunity to be ready for the Kingdom.

6. <u>Matthew 11:9-14</u> **"What did you go out to see? A prophet?**
Yes, I say to you, and more than a prophet.
For this is he of whom it is written: 'Behold, I send My messenger
before Your face, Who will prepare Your way before You.'
Assuredly, I say to you, among those born of women there has not risen
one greater than John the Baptist; but he who is least in the kingdom of
heaven is greater than he.   And from the days of John the Baptist until
now the kingdom of heaven suffers violence, and the violent take it by
force. For all the prophets and the law prophesied until John.
<u>**And if you are willing to receive**</u> (Messiah), <u>**he is Elijah who is to come.**</u>**"**
If Israel was willing to receive MESSIAH and His KINGDOM, then John would
have been Elijah himself, for God would have sent Elijah, and the Kingdom would
have been established soon after, according to the Elijah prophecy.

<u>THE JUDGEMENTS ON THE TEMPLE and JERUSALEM in AD 70 give us some MAJOR PROOFS that JESUS must be the MESSIAH.</u>

1. <u>**Everything Jesus predicted about the destruction of Jerusalem and the Temple and the dispersal of Israel came to pass within 40 years**</u>.
If He was right about that, was He not also right about the cause - Israel's rejection of
Him as the true Messiah?

2. <u>What sin?</u>   Israel's Temple was destroyed and she had to go into a 70 year captivity
to Babylon for the sin of idolatry in 586 BC. Then in 70 AD the Temple was again
destroyed and Israel went into captivity to all nations for 2000 years! The Jews know
that only a terrible sin could cause God to abandon His Temple and allow it to be
destroyed. What sin could possibly account for this? After Babylon, Israel repented of
idolatry but it seems they did something even worse. What is worse than idolatry? None
other than the rejection of Messiah- this was the only possible cause of their destruction.

3. <u>Daniel's 70 Weeks</u> (Daniel 9:24-27) proves that Messiah must have been present
483 years after the command to rebuild Jerusalem (458 BC). It says that Messiah must
come and die: **"the Anointed One will be cut off but not for himself"** (KJV) Another
translation is: **"the Anointed One will be cut off and have nothing"** (NIV) or as the

Living Bible puts it: **"the Anointed One will be killed, His Kingdom still unrealised"** It then predicts the destruction of Jerusalem and the Temple by the Romans. The prophecy makes it clear that final Atonement for Israel's sins had to be made before the 2nd Temple is destroyed. The destruction in AD 70 means Messiah came before then.

4. The Temple Records needed to establish the genealogy of the Messiah were destroyed with the Temple. No one can now prove that they qualify to be the Messiah.

5. Genesis 49:10: **"The sceptre shall not depart from Judah, Nor a lawgiver from between his feet, until Shiloh comes; and to Him shall be the obedience of the people."**
This predicts that two signs would happen soon after the Coming of Messiah (Shiloh):
(1) The removal of Judah's sceptre (tribal staff);
(2) The suppression of the Jewish judicial power.
Even the Talmud said: **"Woe unto us, for the sceptre has been taken from Judah and the Messiah has not appeared."**

6. Haggai 2:6-9 is prophecy that the Second Temple would see a greater glory (Presence of God) than even Solomon's Temple (2 Chronicles 5:14; 7:1-3) and that in it God would grant peace. **"Thus says the LORD of hosts: 'Once more (it is a little while) I will shake heaven and earth, the sea and dry land; and I will shake all nations, and they shall come to the Desire of all Nations, and I will fill this Temple with glory,' says the LORD of hosts. The silver is Mine, and the gold is Mine,' says the LORD of hosts. The glory of this latter Temple shall be greater than the former,' says the LORD of hosts. 'And in this place I will give peace,' says the LORD of hosts."** This can only be true if God Himself in the Person of the Messiah Jesus was in this Temple and offered Himself on Mount Moriah as a sacrifice for us to have peace with God. Since this Temple is now destroyed, this prophecy cannot be fulfilled in any other way.

Malachi 3:1 confirms that the Lord Himself would come to the Second Temple:
"Behold, I send My messenger, and he will prepare the way before Me. And the Lord, whom you seek, will suddenly come to His Temple, even the Messenger of the covenant, in Whom you delight. Behold, He is coming," **says the LORD of hosts"** (see also Psalm 118:26, Zechariah 11:13).

Key 8: The Mystery of the Church.

THE CHURCH WAS A MYSTERY in the Old Testament. The Old Testament prophets saw Christ's first Coming as the Suffering Servant and His Second Coming as King of Kings (and a time of Tribulation just before that) after which the vision of the Old Testament prophets will be fulfilled and God's Kingdom established, but they could not see into the GAP in between - the present Age. They saw Christ would first come and suffer for our sins but it was not clear to them that the Kingdom (Glory) would be postponed for a long time (1Peter 1:10-12). We now know this GAP is about 2000 years long and that God raised up a new group called His CHURCH to be His witness for this Age. However it is clear that the Church was not explicitly mentioned in Old Testament prophecy (it is in the Types, Shadows and Feasts). She was hidden to the Old Testament eye. The CHURCH was not seen or mentioned by the Old Testament prophets. God kept the CHURCH hidden (the prophets saw some events related to Israel at the start and end of this time but not the Church itself. Only when it was clear that Israel was rejecting Christ, was it revealed (by Jesus) that there would be an extended period between the two Comings of Christ and that the responsibility and anointing to guard and spread God's Word would be passed from Israel to the Church for that time. So only when it was clear that Israel was saying 'NO' did God reveal the **MYSTERY** of what would happen between His two Comings.

The Mystery was that there would be a 2000 year GAP and that the CHURCH would fill that gap. **The present Church-Age was a Mystery (Secret) hidden in God, but now revealed in the New Testament.**

One reason that the Church Age was a MYSTERY, only revealed to the apostles when Israel's rejection was clear, is that it can only happen if Israel is cut off and the Kingdom is postponed as Romans 11 makes clear. So, if God revealed it in advance, He could not have made a 'bona fide' (genuine) offer of the Kingdom to Israel at Christ's First Coming. And when He did start to reveal it, it was only secretly to His disciples (mostly through parables - see Matthew 13).

Thus it was explained in a way that the leaders could not understand so that the offer was not compromised (Matthew 13:10-17). So the Church-Age from Pentecost to the Rapture was a mystery hidden in God. (The CHURCH was BORN at PENTECOST - Acts1:5;11:15,16). Thus 'Mystery' is a key word in the New Testament. The 'mysteries' refer to things revealed in the New Testament that were hidden in God in the Old. The word 'Mystery' means 'a Secret' - a word that was used by secret societies having special knowledge possessed only by the initiated members. A mystery was something known to those on the inside but not to those on the outside. Until AD 33 the mystery was hidden in God; that is, the 'society' was the Triune God but now in the Church Age all believers are welcomed into the fellowship of this mystery and can learn the Divine secrets! For believers, a New Testament mystery is a secret revealed.

The Mystery was revealed first by Jesus where He revealed the Mystery Kingdom in parables (Matthew 13).
"All these things Jesus spoke to the multitude in parables; and without a parable He did not speak to them, that it might be fulfilled which was spoken by the prophet, saying: "I will open My mouth in parables; I will utter things kept secret from the foundation of the world" (v34,35).
He prophesied how the KINGDOM would progress IN THE PRESENT MYSTERY AGE. He also predicted that the Holy Spirit would reveal more to the apostles (John 16:12,13).

The full revelation of MYSTERY was given to the Apostle Paul who was especially chosen to reveal the Mystery: **"He is able to establish you according to my gospel and preaching of Jesus Christ, according to the revelation of the mystery kept secret since the world began but now made manifest, and by the prophetic Scriptures made known to all nations"** (Romans 16:25-26).
"I became a minister according to the stewardship from God which was given to me for you, to fulfil (complete) the word of God, the mystery which has been hidden from ages and from generations, but now has been revealed to His saints.
To them God willed to make known what are the riches of the glory of this mystery among the Gentiles: which is Christ in you, the hope of glory" (Colossians 1:25-27).

" I, Paul, the prisoner of Christ Jesus for you Gentiles - if indeed you have heard of the dispensation of the grace of God which was given to me for you, how that <u>by revelation He made known to me the mystery</u> (as I have briefly written already, by which, when you read, you may understand my knowledge in the mystery of Christ), <u>which in other ages was not made known to the sons of men, as it has now been revealed by the Spirit to His holy apostles and prophets:</u> that the Gentiles should be fellow heirs, of the same body, partakers of His promise in Christ through the gospel, of which I became a minister according to the gift of the grace of God given to me by the effective working of His power. To me, who am less than the least of all the saints, this grace was given, that I should preach among the Gentiles the unsearchable riches of Christ, and to make all see what is <u>the fellowship of the mystery, which from the beginning of the ages has been hidden in God</u> who created all things through Jesus Christ" (Ephesians 3:1-10).

Anything called a 'mystery' in the New Testament is something not revealed before the Church Age. The heart of this mystery is the nature of the Church: **"That the Gentiles should be fellow heirs, of the same body, partakers of His promise in Christ through the gospel"** (Ephesians 3:6). The Mystery is not Gentile salvation which happens in every age but that <u>there would be a body of people (distinct from Israel) called the Church where Jew and Gentile have an equal place in one body.</u> Moreover, it would be the BODY and BRIDE of Christ, actually in union with and indwelt by Christ (us in Christ and Christ in us) possessing every New-Covenant blessing (Coloss 1:27, John 14:20).

The mystery was not Messiah's death but it was that Israel would be hardened and cut off, that the Kingdom would be postponed and a new Body would be formed IN CHRIST (where Jew and Gentile, male and female were equal) which would be entrusted with the WORD of GOD and its propagation in this present age instead of Israel. These developments were no surprise to God - they were all in His eternal plan and purpose. Part 2 has more on the Mystery.

Therefore we now have this order of events:
- **THE FIRST COMING OF CHRIST**
- **THE CHURCH AGE**
- **THE SECOND COMING OF CHRIST**
- **THE MILLENNIUM**

Key 9: Prophetic Gaps

Knowing that the Church was a Mystery helps us to understand Old Testament prophecy. The prophets are often talking on a subject and suddenly jump over the Church Age. Sometimes when we look at two hills, one behind the other, we don't see the valley in between, so they didn't know they were jumping across a gap of 2000 years from Christ's First Coming (the Sufferings) to His Second Coming (His Glory). These GAPS wonderfully illustrate that the Church was a mystery hidden in God.

FIRST COMING......(MYSTERY GAP of 2000 years)......SECOND COMING.

There is always a connecting idea that bridges the jump.
(Sometimes because of the common theme there is a similar event on both sides of the GAP and the prophecy can be applied to both sides. When this happens italics are used in the following verses).

1. **The classic example is Isaiah 61:1-3** (Messiah brings in the Jubilee):
"The Spirit of the Lord GOD is upon Me, because the LORD has anointed Me to preach good tidings to the poor; He has sent Me to heal the brokenhearted, to proclaim liberty to the captives, and the opening of the prison to those who are bound; to proclaim the acceptable (Jubilee) **year of the LORD"**
(This was quoted by Jesus in Luke 4:17-20 as being fulfilled by Him right then; however He closed the Book and read no further because He would not fulfil the next part of the scripture for another 2000 years) **...(GAP of 2000 years)...**

"and the day of vengeance of our God (the Second Coming followed by the Millennium); **to comfort all who mourn, to console those who mourn in Zion, to give them beauty for ashes, the oil of joy for mourning, the garment of praise for the spirit of heaviness; that they may be called trees of righteousness, the planting of the LORD, that He may be glorified. And they shall rebuild the old ruins, raise up the former desolations, and repair the ruined cities, the desolations of many generations...."**

The spiritual blessings of v3-11 are a prophecy of the Millennium, but also apply to us in the New Covenant IN CHRIST (Gal 3:26, Romans 11:17). Israel as a nation could have entered their Jubilee in AD33 and seen the whole chapter fulfilled then, because Jesus declared it was Jubilee time ('the acceptable year of the Lord'). But because they rejected it, the Kingdom was postponed and the Mystery Age inserted, which is why the prophecy jumps 2000 years. The Jubilee blessings are available in this Age for individual believers but are only fulfilled for national Israel in the Kingdom.

2. Isaiah 9:6-7: The King and His Kingdom. **"For unto us a Child is born** (His humanity)**, unto us a Son is given** (His Deity)**; and the Government will be upon His shoulder. And His name will be called Wonderful, Counsellor, Mighty God, Father** (Source) **of Eternity, Prince of Peace."**
....(2000 year GAP).... **"Of the increase of His Government and peace there will be no end, upon the throne of David and over His Kingdom, to order it and establish it with judgement and justice, from that time forward, even forever. The zeal of the LORD of hosts will perform this."**

3. Luke 1:31-33 The King and His Kingdom. **"Behold, you will conceive in your womb and bring forth a Son, and shall call His name JESUS. He will be great, and will be called the Son of the Highest"**
.....(2000 year GAP)..... **"and the Lord God will give Him the throne of His father David. And He will reign over the house of Jacob forever, and of His kingdom there will be no end."**

4. Isaiah 11:1-9 The King and Kingdom. **"There shall come forth a Rod from the stem of Jesse, and a Branch shall grow out of his roots. The Spirit of the LORD shall rest upon Him, the Spirit of wisdom and understanding, the Spirit of counsel and might, the Spirit of knowledge and the fear of the LORD. His delight is in the fear of the LORD"** **....(2000 year GAP)....** **"and He shall not judge by the sight of His eyes, nor decide by the hearing of His ears; but with righteousness He shall judge the poor, and decide with equity for the meek of the earth; He shall strike the earth with the rod**

of His mouth, and with the breath of His lips He shall slay the wicked. Righteousness shall be the belt of His loins, and faithfulness the belt of His waist.   The wolf also shall dwell with the lamb, the leopard shall lie down with the young goat, the calf and the young lion and the fatling together; and a little child shall lead them. The cow and the bear shall graze; their young ones shall lie down together; and the lion shall eat straw like the ox. The nursing child shall play by the cobra's hole, and the weaned child shall put his hand in the viper's den. They shall not hurt nor destroy in all My holy mountain, for the earth shall be full of the knowledge of the LORD as the waters cover the sea."

5. Isaiah 40:3-5. The Way Prepared for the King.
"The voice of one crying in the wilderness (John the Baptist): "Prepare the way of the LORD; make straight in the desert a highway for our God" .....(2000 year GAP)...... "Every valley shall be exalted and every mountain and hill brought low; the crooked places shall be made straight and the rough places smooth the glory of the LORD shall be revealed, and all flesh shall see it together; for the mouth of the LORD has spoken."

6. Genesis 49:10. "The sceptre shall not depart from Judah, nor a lawgiver from between his feet, until Shiloh (Messiah) comes" .... (2000 year GAP)...."and to Him shall be the obedience of the people."

7. Micah 5:1-4 The Shepherd-King. "They will strike the Judge of Israel with a rod on the cheek.   But you, Bethlehem Ephrathah, though you are little among the thousands of Judah, yet out of you shall come forth to Me the One to be Ruler in Israel, whose goings forth are from of old, from ever-lasting. Therefore (because Messiah was rejected) He (God) shall give them (Israel) up (in judgement)" ...(2000 year GAP)... "until the time that she who is in labor has given birth; then the remnant of His brethren shall return to the children of Israel. And He (Messiah) shall stand and feed His flock in the strength of the Lord, in the majesty of the Name of the Lord His God; and they shall abide, for now He shall be great to the ends of the earth."

8. Hosea 5:14-6:3. Israel's sin and repentance.

" I (Christ) **will be like a lion to Ephraim, like a young lion to the house of Judah. I, even I, will tear** (cut them off) **and go away** (to Heaven); **I will take them away** (to the nations) **and no one shall rescue. I will return again to My place**" (the Ascension) **...(2000 year GAP).....**

"**till they acknowledge their offence** (of rejecting Him). **Then they will seek My face; in their affliction** (the Tribulation) **they will earnestly seek Me** (saying): "**Come, and let us return to the LORD; for He has torn, but He will heal us; He has stricken, but He will bind us up.   After 2 DAYS** (2000 years) **He will revive us; on the 3RD DAY He will raise us up, that we may live in His sight** (Millennium). **Let us know, let us pursue the knowledge of the LORD.   His going forth** (Second Coming) **is established** (it is as certain) **as the morning** (sunrise); **He will come to us like the rain, like the latter and former rain to the earth** (the outpoured Spirit in the Millennium)"

9. Zechariah 9:9,10. The Presentation of the King.

"**Rejoice greatly, O daughter of Zion!   Shout, O daughter of Jerusalem! Behold, your King is coming to you; He is just and having salvation, lowly and riding on a donkey, a colt, the foal of a donkey**"....**(2000 year GAP)...**

"**I will cut off the chariot from Ephraim and the horse from Jerusalem; the battle bow shall be cut off. He shall speak peace to the nations; His dominion shall be from sea to sea, from the River to the ends of the earth**"

10. Zechariah 13:7. The Sheep (Israel) scattered, because they rejected the Good Shepherd.   "**Awake, O sword, against My Shepherd, against the Man who is My Companion,**" says the LORD of hosts. "**Strike the Shepherd, and the sheep** (Israel) **will be scattered** (Matthew 26:31) **....(2000 year GAP)....** *then I will turn My hand against the little ones* **and it shall come to pass in all the land,**" says the LORD, "**that two-thirds in it shall be cut off and die, but one-third shall be left in it: I will bring the one-third through the fire, refine them as silver is refined, and test them as gold is tested. They will call on My name, and I will answer them.**

I will say, 'This is My people'; and each will say, 'The LORD is my God.'"

11. Malachi 3:1,2 "Behold, I send My messenger (John), and he will prepare the way before Me. And the Lord, whom you seek, will suddenly come to His Temple, even the Messenger of the (New) Covenant, in whom you delight. *Behold, He is coming" says the LORD of hosts"* ....(2000 year GAP).... "But who can endure the day of His Coming? And who can stand when He appears? For He is like a refiner's fire and like launderer's soap. He will sit as a refiner and a purifier of silver; He will purify the sons of Levi, and purge them as gold and silver, that they may offer to the LORD an offering in righteousness. Then the offering of Judah and Jerusalem will be pleasant to the LORD, as in the days of old, as in former years."

12. Revelation 12:1-6 The Rapture of the Man-child. "Now a great sign appeared in heaven: a woman (Israel) clothed with the sun, with the moon under her feet, and on her head a garland of 12 stars. Then being with child (Messiah), she cried out in labour and in pain to give birth. And another sign appeared in heaven: behold, a great, fiery red dragon (satan) having 7 heads and 10 horns, and 7 diadems on his heads. His tail drew a third of the stars of heaven (angels) and threw them to the earth. And the dragon stood before the woman who was ready to give birth, to devour her Child (Jesus) as soon as it was born (the massacre of the innocents at Bethlehem). She bore a male Child who was to rule all nations with a rod of iron, *and her Child was caught up to God and His throne"* .... (2000 year GAP)...."Then the woman fled into the wilderness, where she has a place prepared by God, that they should feed her there 1260 days" (this happens in the Tribulation). The link here is the catching up of Christ to the Throne. First the Head (Christ) in AD 33, then the Body (the Church in Christ) 2000 years later Then comes the events of the Tribulation. So when Christ and the Church are removed from the earth, the devil centres all his attack on Israel to destroy her.

13. Daniel 9:25-27. Jerusalem and the Temple. "From the going forth of the command to restore and build Jerusalem (458 BC) until Messiah the

Prince, there shall be **7 Weeks** (49 years) **and 62 Weeks** (434 years); **the street shall be built again, and the wall, even in the narrow time** (the 49 years). **After the 62 weeks** (sometime after 483 years) **Messiah shall be cut off, but not for Himself; and** <u>the people of the prince who is to come</u> (the Romans) **shall destroy the city and the sanctuary. The end of it shall be with a flood, and until the end of the war desolations are determined"** (fulfilled in AD 67-73). **.... (2000 year GAP).....**

<u>**"Then he**</u> (the Roman prince to come) **shall confirm a covenant with the majority for one Week** (the 7 year Tribulation) **but in the middle of the Week, he shall bring an end to sacrifice and offering. And on a wing of the Temple he will set up an Abomination that causes desolation** (desecrating the Temple by setting up his own image to be worshipped), **even until the consummation determined, is poured out on the desolator"** (Jesus destroys antichrist at His Return). The connecting link is the Roman Empire for they destroyed Jerusalem in the first century and are called 'the people of the prince who is to come.' Thus after the 2000 years we see the Prince of a Revived Rome making a covenant with Israel that starts the final 7-year Tribulation.

14. Daniel 11:35-36 The Antichrist. v21-35 has been fulfilled in Antiochus the Great - a type of Antichrist 175-163 BC. Then the prophecy jumps to the antichrist himself **..... (2000 year GAP)... "then the king** (antichrist) **shall do according to his own will: he shall exalt and magnify himself above every god, shall speak blasphemies against the God of gods, and shall prosper till the wrath has been accomplished; for what has been determined shall be done"** (Daniel 11:36- 12:1 give events in the future Tribulation).

15. Daniel 7:23-27. The Roman Empire which dominated Israel will be revived in the end-times. **"The 4th beast shall be a 4th kingdom on earth** (Rome), **which shall be different from all other kingdoms, *and shall devour the whole earth, trample it and break it in pieces* ....(2000 year GAP).... The ten horns are ten kings who shall arise from this kingdom** (the Revived Rome). **And another** (the antichrist) **shall rise after them; he shall be**

different from the first ones, and shall subdue three kings. He shall speak
pompous words against the Most High, shall persecute the saints of the
Most High, and shall intend to change times and law. Then the saints
shall be given into his hand for a Time, Times and half a Time (the Great
Tribulation). But the court (in Heaven) shall be seated, and they shall take
away his dominion, to consume and destroy it forever. Then the kingdom
and dominion, and the greatness of the kingdoms under the whole heaven
shall be given to the people, the saints of the Most High.
His Kingdom is an everlasting Kingdom, and all dominions shall serve
and obey Him (God's Kingdom established)."

16. Daniel 2:32-35.
"This image's head *was* of fine gold, its chest and arms of silver,
its belly and thighs of bronze, its legs of iron (Rome)
....(2000 year GAP)...
its feet partly of iron and partly of clay (Revived Rome).
You watched while a stone was cut out without hands, which struck
the image on its feet of iron and clay, and broke them in pieces.
Then the iron, clay, bronze, silver, and gold were crushed together,
and became like chaff from the summer threshing floors; the wind carried
them away so that no trace of them was found. The stone that struck the
image became a great mountain and filled the whole earth."

17. Isaiah 49:1-13. Jesus speaks towards the end of His ministry concerning
God's salvation going also to the Gentiles:
"Listen, O coast lands, to Me, and take heed, you peoples from afar!
The LORD has called Me from the womb; from the matrix of My mother He
has made mention of My name.   He has made My mouth like a sharp
sword; in the shadow of His hand He has hidden Me, and made Me a
polished shaft; in His quiver He has hidden Me. And He said to me,
'You are My servant, O Israel, in whom I will be glorified.'
Then I (Jesus) said, 'I have laboured in vain,
I have spent my strength for nothing and in vain (because it seems Israel

was rejecting Him and the Kingdom is not going to be established),
yet surely my just reward is with the LORD, and my work with my God.'

And now the LORD says, Who formed Me from the womb to be His Servant, to bring Jacob back to Him, so that Israel is gathered to Him (for I shall be glorious in the eyes of the LORD, and My God shall be My strength) (His first mission was to Israel). **Indeed He says, 'It is too small a thing that You should be My Servant to raise up the tribes of Jacob, and to restore the preserved ones of Israel;** <u>**I will also give You as a Light to the Gentiles, that You should be My salvation to the ends of the earth'**</u> (God reveals an extension of His mission, that through Israel's rejection salvation will go to the Gentiles).

Thus says the LORD, the Redeemer of Israel, their Holy One, to Him whom man despises, to Him whom the nation (Israel) **abhors, to the Servant of rulers: "(Gentile) Kings shall see and arise, princes also shall worship, because of the LORD who is faithful, the Holy One of Israel; and He has chosen You." Thus says the LORD: "In an acceptable time I have heard you, and in the day of salvation I have helped you"** (quoted in 2 Corinthians 6:2 - this is the Jubilee message now preached to the Gentiles)
...(2000 year GAP)...
<u>The KINGDOM</u>: **"I will preserve You and give you as a covenant to the people, to restore the earth, to cause them to inherit the desolate heritages; that You may say to the prisoners 'Go forth,' to those who are in darkness, 'Show yourselves.' They shall feed along the roads, and their pastures shall be on all desolate heights. They shall neither hunger nor thirst, neither heat nor sun shall strike them; for He who has mercy on them will lead them, even by the springs of water He will guide them. I will make each of My mountains a road, and My highways shall be elevated. Surely these shall come from afar; Look! Those from the north and west, and these from the land of Sinim." Sing O heavens! Be joyful O earth! and break out in singing, O mountains! For the LORD has comforted His people, mercy on His afflicted."**

17. Isaiah 28;16: "Therefore thus says the Lord GOD: "Behold, I lay in Zion (1) a STONE for a Foundation, a tried STONE** (the Messiah in His First Coming who would be tried and tested, and through his death and resurrection would lay the foundation for our salvation and for His Kingdom, see Zech 3:9) **..(2000 years)..(2) a precious Cornerstone** (really the Cap or Pinnacle STONE) **(a sure foundation; whoever believes** (in the Foundation Stone) **will not act hastily** (will not be in fear)." The One who became the Foundation Stone in His 1st Coming, will also be manifested as the Capstone (the supreme ruling Stone) in His 2nd Coming. He is both: **"(1) a STONE of Stumbling, and (2) a ROCK of Falling"** (Isaiah 8:14,15; also Romans 9:33,10:11). **"(1) The Stone the builders rejected** (1st Coming) **has (2) become the Chief** (Head or Pinnacle) **Stone** (to be fully manifested at His Second Coming)" (Psa118:22, Mark 12:10, Acts 4:11).

Christ is both the first (foundation) stone and the last (the chief, head or pinnacle Stone). He is both the lowest (laying the foundation through His sufferings) and the highest (in His glory, exalted, enthroned over all, the Chief Stone).   As far as the Church is concerned He is already the Chief (Head) Stone as well as the Foundation Stone (Eph 2:20). As far as Israel and the Kingdom is concerned He is yet to be put into place as the Capstone at His Return. The New Testament Commentary on these verses agrees with this 2-fold fulfilment:

1Peter 2:4-8: **"Come to Him *as to* a living Stone, rejected indeed by men, but chosen by God *and* precious.... Therefore it is also contained in the Scripture** (Isa 28:16), *"Behold, I lay in Zion (1) a Stone, (2) a Chief (Cap) Stone, elect, precious, and he who believes on Him will by no means be put to shame."* **Therefore, to you who believe** *He is* **precious; but to those who are disobedient,** *"(1) The* (Foundation) *Stone that the builders rejected (2) has become the Chief Stone (Capstone)"* **and** *"(1) A Stone that makes them stumble and (2) a Rock of offense* (a Rock that makes them fall)." **They stumble, being disobedient to the word."**   (1) Christ, as the First (Foundation) Stone has already come down (1st Coming), but unbelievers who come across Him but continue to walk in their own ways (rather than standing on Him) stumble over Him and fall. (2) Christ, the Chief Stone, will also come down from above (His 2nd Coming) and fall upon His enemies and crush them in judgement (Daniel 2:34,35,44,45) Christ presented these 2 contrasting images of the same Stone in Matt 21;42,44 (Lk 20:17,18): **"Have you never read in the Scriptures: (1)** *The stone which the builders rejected* **has (2) become the Chief (Cap)Stone. This is the Lord's doing, and it is marvelous in our eyes? And (1) whoever falls** (stumbles) **on this Stone will be broken to pieces; but (2) on whoever it falls, it will grind** (crush) **him to powder."** (See Zechariah 4:7-9 for a type of these 2 Stones)

Key 10: The Tribulation

The prophets saw the First and Second Comings of Messiah (the Sufferings and the Glory) but not the time in between which was a MYSTERY to them. They also saw that just prior to the Second Coming there would be a special time of unparalled evil and distress on earth and for Israel in particular, that would be unique in all of history. **"At that time...there shall be a Time of Trouble** (Tribulation) **such as never was since there was a nation, even to that time** (the GREAT TRIBULATION). **And at that time your people shall be delivered, every one who is found written in the Book** (an escape from the antichrist will be provided to believers in israel). **And** (at the end of this time of Tribulation at the Return of Christ) **many of those who sleep in the dust of the earth shall awake .... to everlasting life"** (Daniel 12:1,2).

Jeremiah 30:3-11 describes this time as **'the time of Jacob's Trouble'** that happens just before Israel is restored and the Kingdom is established:

"For behold, the days are coming,' says the Lord, `that I will bring back from captivity My people Israel and Judah,' says the Lord. "And I will cause them to return to the land that I gave to their fathers, and they shall possess it." (this has been fulfilled in recent times - 1948).

The Tribulation: **"Now these are the words that the Lord spoke concerning Israel and Judah. For thus says the Lord: `We have heard a voice of trembling, of fear, and not of peace. Ask now, and see, whether a man is ever in labour with child? So why do I see every man with his hands on his loins like a woman in labour, and all faces turned pale? Alas! For that Day** (of the Lord) **is great, so that none is like it; and it is the time of Jacob's Trouble, but he shall be saved out of it. For it shall come to pass in that Day,' says the Lord of hosts, `That I will break his yoke from your neck, and will burst your bonds; foreigners shall no more enslave them."**

This is followed by the Millennium: **"But they shall serve the LORD their God, and David their king whom I will raise up for them. Therefore do not fear O My servant Jacob' says the LORD, `Nor be dismayed, O Israel; for behold, I will save you from afar, and your seed from the land of their captivity. Jacob shall return, have rest and be quiet, and no one shall** make him afraid. For I am with you,' says the LORD, `to save you; though I make a full end of all nations where I have scattered you, yet I will not make a complete end of you. But I will correct you in justice, and will not let you go altogether unpunished."

We shall see that 2Thessalonians 2 and Revelation 4-18 confirms that after the Church Age, evil is allowed to come to it's fullness (through the antichrist) and God's wrath is poured out on earth as He begins to deal with the wicked systems of the world. So this period of time is a special time of Divine Judgement called **the TRIBULATION** and **the DAY OF THE LORD.** It is the climax in the war between good and evil. God's intervention is completed by the Return of the Messiah to destroy all evildoers from the earth and establish His Kingdom. **This time is brought to an end by the Return of Christ** (2Thess 2:8, Revelation19)

We shall see the origin of the Tribulation in the prophecy of Daniel's 70 Weeks (9:24-27). It tells us that it will be 7 years long (the 70th Week, v27), divided into 2 halves (confirmed in Revelation by the repeated references to periods of 3.5 years). The 2nd half being worse is called the Great Tribulation, and is initiated by antichrist's breaking of his covenant with Israel, capturing the Temple Mount and putting up his Abomination of Desolation there. Soon after he sets up his world-dictatorship enforced by the mark of the beast (Rev 13). Israel are told to escape at this time to a place where God will protect them (Matthew 24:15-22, Rev 12). The reason for the future 7 year Tribulation under antichrist is Israel's rejection of Christ after 7 years of grace (the original 70th Week AD26-33). These 7 years are rerun as a time of judgement, but they also give Israel a 2nd chance to receive the King and His Kingdom, which she does by calling on the Name of the Lord Jesus Christ to save her from antichrist at the battle of Armageddon.

So the Prophets saw:
1. **THE FIRST COMING OF CHRIST** (in humility
- His birth, death and resurrection - as the LAMB OF GOD).
2. **A MYSTERY TIME** (the present Age)
3. **The TRIBULATION** (a relatively short time, 7 years, of judgement)
4. **The SECOND COMING OF CHRIST** (in glory, as KING of KINGS)
5. **THE MESSIANIC KINGDOM** (the Golden Age).
This gives us our basic framework for understanding prophecy.

Key 11: The Framework Prophecies

There are three Bible prophecies that have special importance because they provide a overall framework for end-time prophecy. Understanding these is necessary, because only when once the framework is up, we can start to fit the other prophecies into place.

1. **Daniel 9:24-27 (Daniel's Seventy Weeks)**
2. **Matthew 24   (The Olivet Discourse)**
3. **The Book of Revelation.**

Framework Prophecy 1 - Daniel's 70 Weeks (Daniel 9:24-27)

is a major key to prophecy and is the lynch-pin connecting Old and New Testament prophecy, preparing us for the New developments. It is a good example of the GAP principle (Key 8) and establishes the postponement of the Kingdom (crucial to relating Old Testament prophecy and the Church Age). It also proves that despite the delay, the Kingdom will be established and Israel will be fully restored. It's a MASTERPIECE OF PROPHECY. The end-time prophecy of Jesus (the Olivet Discourse) depends and builds upon it. It gives a countdown to the Kingdom! Before Abraham, was the time (dispensation) of the Gentiles (2000 years). From Abraham was the time of Israel. Now Israel was in dispersion in Babylon and Daniel was praying about the restoration of Israel - her people from sin and her city from desolation (Daniel 9). God's answer gives a prophecy giving the timing of the restoration in terms of 'Weeks'. A 'Week' means a 'Seven'. It can mean a week of days or a week of years. From the context it is generally accepted that Daniel's 70 Weeks are Weeks of years and so refer to 70 Sevens of years or 490 years. If days had been intended it would be so expressed, as in Daniel 10:3 which literally says 'three whole weeks of days'. Moreover the last Week is divided into two, and the second half is three and a half years (Daniel 7:25, 12:7; Revelation 11:2,3).

God's answer to Daniel comes in v24:

"70 Weeks (Sevens) **are determined** (cut, marked and divided off)
for your people (Israel) **and for your holy city** (Jerusalem)."

Now God gives six things that will be accomplished by the end of this time.
The first three have to do with sin, the second three with the Kingdom.
Before the Kingdom can be established the issue of sin had to be dealt with
and provision for man's righteousness made through the New Covenant:

"(1) To finish the transgression
(2) To make an end of sins
(3) To make reconciliation (atonement) **for iniquity."**

These first three were fulfilled by Christ when He died on the Cross, bearing
the judgment for our sins, laying the basis for us to be part of His Kingdom.
As Christ declared "it is finished - the price is paid in full", He was claiming
the fulfilment of this first stage towards establishing the Kingdom.

On the basis of Christ's death God can establish the Millennial Kingdom:
(4) To bring in everlasting righteousness (or 'the age of righteousness')
(5) To seal up vision and prophecy (to bring all old Testament prophecy
to fulfilment. This will only be true in the Millennium).
(6) To anoint the Most Holy" (the establishing and anointing of the Millennial
Temple for the Messianic Kingdom - see Ezekiel 41-46).

These final three things will only be fulfilled by Christ when He comes again and
establishes the Kingdom on earth. Together the six describe God's whole
program to bring Israel into all the blessings promised in the covenants. This
includes personal salvation through the new-covenant and the establishment
of the Kingdom on earth under the personal rule of the Son of David from
Jerusalem. When Israel accepts the work of Christ in fulfilling the first three,
Christ can complete God's plan to restore Israel by fulfilling the next three.

This amazing prophecy says that God has set aside 490 years for Israel to be
fully restored, for the prophesied Kingdom of God to be established on earth.

Thus, Israel has only 490 years left 'on her clock' to possess the Kingdom.

v25: **"Know therefore and understand that..."**
(This is a hard prophecy that demands an effort on our part to study and understand it, as Jesus confirmed in Matthew 24:15)
"from the going forth of the command to restore and rebuild Jerusalem..."
This gives the starting point - the decree of Artaxerxes to Ezra in 458 BC
(for justification of this starting date, see pages 108-110).
"...until MESSIAH THE PRINCE." The 490 years close with the time of
'Messiah the Prince'. Notice that He is not described as 'Messiah the King' at this stage, but 'Messiah the Prince' (the King in waiting), for His ministry first of all must be to do what is necessary for His Kingdom to be established on earth. In particular He must achieve the spiritual restoration of Israel (for the Messianic Kingdom must be centred upon Israel). Then He can reign as Messiah the King. v25 reveals that the full restoration described in v24 will be fulfilled by MESSIAH, for it is He who must establish the Kingdom. He will come first to Israel as their Prince, and when they receive Him, He will become their King. The end-point of the prophecy (490 years from 458 BC) is AD 33 - the year of the Cross! This implies that Jesus was ready to establish the Kingdom in that year.

Next Daniel gives us a breakdown of the 490 years:
"Until MESSIAH THE PRINCE there shall be 7 weeks (7 sevens= 49 years)
and 62 weeks (434 years). **The street shall be rebuilt again and the wall even in troublesome times"** (or 'the narrow time' - this was fulfilled in the first 49 years -see the book of Ezra-Nehemiah).

The time of Messiah's Presentation to Israel starts after the 49 + 434 = 483 years. Therefore the end of the 483 years (AD 26) is the start of the time of Messiah's Presentation to Israel. This leaves the MESSIAH just 7 years to fulfil the prophecy, which predicts that after 490 years have been fulfilled, the Kingdom Age should be established, which will be the time of 'Messiah the King.' These 7 final years of Daniel's prophecy, the time of Messiah the Prince and His ministry to Israel, should begin in AD26 and end in AD 33 (according to Daniel).

The New Testament record makes it clear that the formal start of the time of Messiah, was when His herald John the Baptist began his ministry to Israel. The Gospels all start the story of Christ's ministry and presentation to Israel with the ministry of John the Baptist (Luke 3 for example). Jesus confirmed that John brought in the time of the Messiah (Matthew 11:9-13) saying: **"all the prophets prophesied unto John."** John signalled the start of the fulfilment of Messianic prophecy, the Appearance of the Messiah (Isaiah 40:3-5, Matthew 3:3). It was starting with his ministry that **"the Kingdom of God was at hand"** (Matthew 3:2) Moreover Acts 1:21,22 defines the time of Messiah as: **"the time that the Lord Jesus went in and out among us'**, as: **'beginning from the Baptism of John to that day when He was taken up from us** (the Ascension)**."** The 'baptism of John' refers to his whole mission (Matthew 21:25). Thus the fulfilment of Daniel's prophecy requires the start of John's ministry to be in AD26.

This significant date is confirmed by the New Testament record. In fact the start of John's ministry is the most strongly emphasised date of the New Testament: **"Now in the 15th year of the reign of Tiberius Caesar, Pontius Pilate being governor of Judea (AD 26-36), Herod being tetrarch of Galilee, his brother Philip tetrarch of Iturea and the region of Trachonitis, and Lysanias tetrarch of Abilene, while Annas and Caiaphas were high priests, the word of God came to John the son of Zacharias in the wilderness"** (Luke 3:1,2). This is the key date marking a new phase in God's plan. Bible Chronology hinges on this date because it marks the close of Daniel's 69th Week and the opening of the ministry of Messiah when the Kingdom was at hand. Now Tiberius Caesar began ruling as co-emperor with Augustus in AD12 and ruled alone from AD14-37. Now the word used for his 'reign' is 'hegemonia' (rulership or leadership) rather than 'basileia' (the usual word used for the sole 'reign' of a king). Thus his 'hegemonia' began in AD12 and his 15th year was AD 26. Thus is John the Baptist started announcing the Messiah at the very time Daniel had predicted the start of the time of Messiah's coming to Israel!

Thus Daniel predicted that the time of 'Messiah the Prince' starts after 483 years (fulfilled in the ministry of John starting in AD26) and ends after 490 years (fulfilled in the death of the Messiah Jesus in AD 33). Since we know that Jesus' ministry lasted 3.5 years (AD 29-33), we can conclude that John's ministry was also 3.5 years (AD 26-29). This is confirmed by the 7 years of the Tribulation (likewise divided in two halves) which as we shall see is a rerun of these 7 years.

The death of Christ in AD 33 is widely accepted, and is also confirmed by secular historical writings that describe the supernatural darkness that covered the world at that time. Moreover only AD 30 and 33 satisfy the criteria of a Friday full moon as required for the Passover in the year of the Cross. However, some prefer AD 30 because it has been popular to believe that Christ was born in 4 BC, because it was thought that Josephus gave this date for Herod's death. Since Jesus was about 30 when He started His ministry of 3.5 years, this would give AD 30 as the year of the Cross. However recent scholarship has shown that Josephus has been misinterpreted, and that Herod's death was in 1BC, and Christ's birth was in 2BC (which confirms 33 AD for the Cross, since there is no year 0). This agrees with the consistent witness of the Church Fathers who had access to better information. This is all well documented in the revised edition of Finegan's 'Handbook of Biblical Chronology'.
In conclusion, we have good evidence that John's ministry began in AD 26, and the Cross was in AD 33. This means that the 7 years predicted by Daniel as the time of 'Messiah the Prince' (AD 26-33) was fulfilled in the 7 years of the messianic ministry of John and Jesus.

Sometime after the 483 years - after Messiah's Presentation begins, the Messiah is to be killed for us:
v26 **"And after the 62 weeks MESSIAH shall be cut off - but not for himself."** We have seen that at the end of the 62 weeks the Messianic ministry would begin. Now we are told that sometime later, at the end of this ministry the Messiah would be killed, not for His own sins but for ours. In fact, we now know that it was after seven years, at the end of the Seventy Weeks in AD 33, that Messiah was killed (as v24 implied). We know from the Feasts and Seasons described in John's Gospel and from Luke 13:7 that Jesus ministered for three and a half years. So John must have ministered for the three and a half years before that, typified by Elijah's ministry (James 5:17). (This pattern of the 70th Week divided into two halves is confirmed when we see it repeated in the 7-year Tribulation, when the 70th Week is rerun). The prophecy is strangely silent

about these seven years of Messiah (Daniel's 70th Week) after which the Kingdom should have been established. These most important years are left blank, except for the mention of Messiah's substitutionary death at their end.

According to v24, by the end of the 70th Week (AD33), Jesus Christ should have died for our sins and established the Kingdom. He did die and establish the New Covenant in His Blood, and He was ready to establish the Kingdom that year and fulfil the prophecy of the 490 years, but something happens to delay this, which is anticipated in the prophecy in v26.

First: **"Messiah will be cut off but not for himself"** (KJV) could also be translated: **"the Anointed One will be cut off and have nothing"** (NIV) or as the Living Bible puts it: **"the Anointed One will be killed, His Kingdom still unrealised."** For some reason the Kingdom does not come after 490 years!

Then as the prophecy in v26 continues, there's another strange development. Instead of Messiah establishing the Kingdom we find:
"and the people (the Romans) **of the prince who is to come shall destroy the city and the sanctuary. The end of it shall be with a flood and until the end of the war desolations are determined"** (fulfilled in the war of AD 66-73 when Rome destroyed Jerusalem and scattered Israel to the nations). Something has gone terribly wrong! Such destruction and judgement on Israel could only mean Israel will reject her Messiah!
(This couldn't have been said explicitly without spoiling their freedom of choice). So the Kingdom could not come at the end of the 490 years!

But how will God fulfil the prophecy of 490 years, as He must?

Praise God Who: **"changes the times and the seasons"** (Daniel 2:20-22). God does something special with the last seven years on Israel's Timetable, about which, so far, the prophecy has been silent. Because they rejected their King and Kingdom, He officially cut them off (Luke 13:4-8, Acts 7), stopped their clock and cancelled their last 7 years (AD 26-33, the time of Messiah's

Presentation). This is why the 7 years, AD 26-33 are blotted out of v26. He will give them a second chance by letting the seven years (Daniel's 70th Week) run again for Israel at the end of the age, after which Christ returns to establish the Kingdom and is received by a believing Israel. The difference is that these are 7 years of Tribulation under antichrist, rather than 7 years of Grace under Christ. In the first 7 years Christ presented Himself as King, but in the last seven years antichrist will present himself as king. Both seven-year periods divide into two halves, where things that begin in the first half come to their climax in the second half.   Thus v24 will still be literally fulfilled, because the Kingdom will be established after 490 years on Israel's clock. However before the final 7 years on Israel's clock run, the 2000 years or so of the Church-Age are inserted which delay the coming of the Kingdom.   So there is a GAP between the two sets of 7 years filled by the Church-Age (not mentioned because it is a Mystery).

The precedent and type for this is the dreams of Pharaoh in the time of JOSEPH (Genesis 41) where 7 lean cows eat 7 fat ones and 7 thin, blighted heads of grain eat up 7 good heads.   This referred to 7 prosperous years being EATEN UP by 7 years of famine and affliction which came after. So the 7 blessed years of John and Christ were 'eaten up' (blotted out) on Israel's calendar and replaced by 7 years of TRIBULATION by the end of which the Kingdom must be established.   Joseph is a type of Christ and his brothers are Israel. The brothers rejected Joseph as their leader and 'killed' him. They did not come to him in the first 7 years but in the years of Tribulation ('the time of Jacob's trouble' - Jer 30:7); they realised their trouble was due to their sin against Joseph and were repentant.   After testing them, Joseph revealed himself to his brothers in the 7 years of Tribulation and they were reconciled.   Likewise, Jesus will reveal Himself to Israel and they will be reconciled and receive Him as their King.

Verses 26,27 describe two consequences of Israel's rejection of her Prince.
(1) The first judgement came to that generation: **"the people of the prince who is to come** (the Romans) **shall destroy the city and the sanctuary.
The end of it** (the city) **shall be with a flood** (an overwhelming invasion) **and until the end of the war desolations are determined"** (v26).

This took place over a 7-year period from AD 66-73.

<u>(2) The second judgement is the coming of a future prince</u>: 'the prince who is to come', who is of the Roman Empire (for v26 says that his people are the ones who destroy Jerusalem and the Temple).   His destructive activities against Jerusalem and the Temple also take place over a 7-year period (the Tribulation - Daniel's 70th Week). They are described in v27 and identify him as the antichrist.   This shows that the antichrist will be the head of a Revived Roman Empire.   There is a contrast between two princes (who both aspire to be world-rulers).   There is the Jewish 'Messiah the Prince' (the Christ) and the Roman 'prince to come' (the antichrist). Because Israel rejected her true Messiah-Prince after 7-years of grace, she must endure life under the false Messiah-Prince for the 7-year Tribulation. Thus the cause of the Tribulation is Israel's rejection of her Messiah and the rerunning of Daniel's 70th Week.

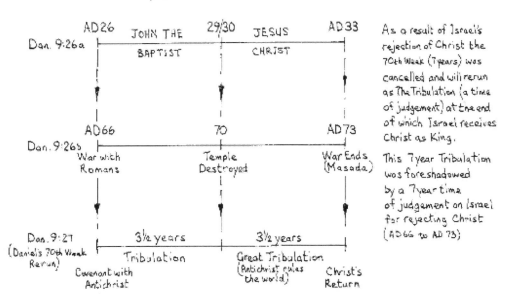

After v26, the prophecy jumps forward to these last seven years for Israel.
After introducing the Roman prince in v26 as an important figure yet to come,

<u>v27 tells us more about him</u>: **"Then** (after an undisclosed period of time) **he** (this must be the last person mentioned - 'the prince who is to come', the antichrist) **shall confirm a covenant** (peace-treaty) **with the many** (the majority in Israel) **for ONE WEEK** (7 years!)."   Here we see Daniel's 70th Week (the last 7-years before the Kingdom comes).   It is marked by the activity of the antichrist. The starting point for these seven years of Tribulation is a peace treaty he makes with Israel as part of his rise to world-power.   This agreement may promise Israel protection, allowing them to worship in a rebuilt Temple.

"But in the middle of the Week (after 3 and a half years, at Mid-Tribulation) **he will bring an end to sacrifice and offering."**
He will break this covenant, invade Jerusalem and stop their Temple worship.
"And one who causes desolation (either antichrist or his assistant - the False-prophet, see Rev 13) **will place abominations on a wing of the Temple..."**
This is the 'abomination of desolation' that Jesus refers to in Matthew 24:15. Antichrist will utterly defile the sanctuary of God by putting an idol of himself on the pinnacle and in the holy-of-holies of the rebuilt Jewish Temple and demand that everyone worship him.   This desolation will continue: "...**until the end** (of the 70th Week) **- the time God has set, to pour out judgement on this evil desolator."** This time is limited to three and a half years, after which antichrist and his kingdom will be destroyed.   <u>This must be accomplished by the return of the Kingly Messiah, Jesus Christ at the end of the 7 years to deliver His people and to establish His Kingdom thus fulfilling the 490-year prophecy.</u>
This agrees with prophecies in Daniel 2 and 7.

<u>There are two 7-year judgements upon Israel for her 7-year rejection of Christ</u> (AD 26-33). The first (v26), was fulfilled in AD 66-73, exactly 40 years later. This was a forerunner of the second (v27) - the future Tribulation.   They have interesting parallels. Both increase in severity with time. Both see a Roman invasion of Jerusalem half-way through the 7-years, followed by a desecration or destruction of the Temple.   The second-half is a time of great tribulation and by the end of 7-years the nation of Israel is at the point of extinction.   In the Olivet Discourse, Jesus basically expounds and expands upon this prophecy of Daniel.

In so doing he predicts the invasion of Jerusalem in AD 70 (Luke 21:20-24, c.f Daniel 9:26) and the parallel invasion in theTribulation (Matthew 24:15-22, c.f. Daniel 9:27). In so doing he brings out another similarity - that in both cases a way of escape will be made for believers just before destruction hits. Because of these similarities many think these are identical events but there are also clear differences. The invasion in Luke results in desolation and captivity in the nations for a long period of time (v24). Thus, Jesus predicts an invasion well before the end of the age in line with Daniel 9:26. On the other hand the invasion in Matthew results in the desecration (not the total destruction) of the Temple and it happens just before Christ's Return (v22-31). Thus Jesus also predicted a second invasion very near the end, in line with Daniel 9:27.

Jesus also warned of these coming Roman judgements in Luke 23:26-31:

"As they led Him away, they laid hold of a certain man, Simon a Cyrenian, who was coming from the country, and on him they laid the cross that he might bear *it* **after Jesus. And a great multitude of the people followed Him, and women who also mourned and lamented Him. But Jesus, turning to them, said, "Daughters of Jerusalem, do not weep for Me, but weep for yourselves and for your children. For indeed the days are coming in which they will say, `Blessed** *are* **the barren, wombs that never bore, and breasts which never nursed!' Then they will begin `to say to the mountains, "Fall on us!" and to the hills, "Cover us! For if they do these things in the green wood** (in a time of grace), **what will be done in the dry** (in a time of judgement)**?"**

Between v26 and v27, Daniel's prophecy jumps 2000 years or so. It is a good example of a Prophetic Gap. The connecting link is Rome and the Roman Prince, identified by the phrase: **'the people of the prince to come'**. At the end of the first run of Daniel's 70th Week, Israel rejected Christ as their ruler, saying that "Caesar is our King" and the Roman army destroyed Jerusalem soon after (v26). Appropriately, the last 7 years open with Israel receiving the antichrist as ruler. v26 describes him as the Coming Prince whose people destroyed Jerusalem in AD 70. This shows he is head of a Revived Roman Empire. v27 describes the continuing judgement and destruction that will come on Israel through Rome for rejecting Christ and accepting the wrong ruler, but at the end of it they will be ready to accept the true Christ (v24).

The rerun of Daniel's 70th Week (the Tribulation) has many parallels with the 70th Week cancelled by God (AD26-33). One opens with the presentation of Christ to Israel, the other with antichrist. Satan tempts each man with world-power mid-way through the 7 years. One rejects, one accepts. At this point both are filled with supernatural power to fulfil their missions- one (possessed) by satan, the other (anointed) by God, launching them to prominence requiring everyone to decide to believe or reject them. At the close of both Weeks Israel has a decision to accept or reject her Messiah. The first time she says 'no', but the second time she will say 'yes'. The first 70th Week ended with the death of Christ (v26), but the second Week finishes with the destruction of anti-christ (v27). The first time the only first 3 points of v24 were fulfilled, the second time the last 3 will be also.

This chronology of Daniel's prophecy differs from the better known calculation done by Sir Robert Anderson. He takes 445 BC (the royal command to Nehemiah in the 20th year of Artaxerxes) as the starting point and uses years of 360 days. He views the 69 Weeks as ending at Jesus' triumphal entry into Jerusalem in 32 AD, and the 70th Week as postponed because of Israel's rejection. The effective differences with the interpretation that I propose (which derive from the insights of Sir Edward Denney) are subtle but important (see Appendix)

I have come to see Denney's view as superior for the following reasons:

(1) It is generally accepted that the Cross was in AD 33 (or 30) but certainly not AD 32. For this reason H.Hoehner has adapted Anderson's dates by a year (from 444 BC-AD 33).

(2) The Year-Length in use by Israel at that time was the luni-solar year which approximates to our solar year in average length. It was not the Gentile (Babylonian) Time of 360 days. Israel's Clock would not using this year. There are special times when a 360 day year is used in the Bible (at the Flood and in the Tribulation -both times of world-wide judgement), however to call it a 'prophetic year' (as if it was the year always used in prophecy) is misleading. When Daniel spoke of 490 years it would be assumed he was referring to the standard year used by Israel. So Anderson's use of this unusual year length is a weakness.

(3) The death and resurrection of Christ must happen on a Jubilee.
In fact at the end of 490 years it happened at the end of a Great Jubilee.

(4) God's offer of the Kingdom to Israel was genuine. Therefore, had Israel accepted, the Kingdom would have had to have been established later in AD 33 (the year of the Cross), fulfilling the 70 Weeks prophecy on time. This requires the 70 Weeks to end in AD33. When Israel failed the 70th Week was cancelled to be rerun as the Tribulation.

(5) The start of Daniel's Seventy Weeks:
"The commandment ('dabar' = 'word from God') **to restore and build Jerusalem."**

POSSIBILITIES: There are 4 to consider, but I believe the decree in 458 BC is the correct one.

(A) The Decree of Cyrus 536 BC (Ezra 1:2-4).   This concerns the Temple alone -
it does not mention Jerusalem as such. Now Isaiah 44:28,45:13 seems to include
Jerusalem in his decree but actually it is God who speaks His purposes to Cyrus,
Jerusalem and the Temple and all four of these decrees are manifestations of this.
However the part of it that came through Cyrus clearly concerned the Temple alone.

(B) The Decree of Darius 518 BC (Ezra 6:1-3). This just renews Cyrus' Temple Decree.

(C) Artaxerxes Decree in his 7th year. 458 BC (Ezra 7:11-26). This clearly had a Divine origin
as the word 'commandment' implies (v6,27). The later Decree by Artaxerxes in 445BC was
in response to Nehemiah's request rather than a direct 'word from God.'
Moreover the Bible emphasises this decree by: (1) having a chapter devoted to it,
with a detailed copy given which shows it to fit Daniel's prophecy.
(2) it is central to the book of Ezra-Nehemiah for all its events originate from it.
(3) its date is emphasised strongly (v7-9).   (4) it is the only bit of Ezra in Aramaic not Hebrew.

Now on the surface this decree seems to emphasise the Temple and thus it not qualify,
but a closer reading shows clearly that this decree included the rebuilding of city and its
administration.   It empowered him to ordain laws, set magistrates and judges with authority
to punish. So Ezra was authorised to restore the commonwealth and the means were placed
at his disposal to enable him to do so. This must be the decree to rebuild and restore
Jerusalem and this is seen to be Ezra's understanding of it.

Ezra 1-6 describes the rebuilding of the Temple before Ezra, except for a parenthesis in Ezra
4:6-23 where in describing resistance to this work Ezra then also describes the resistance
he faced in his time. This section shows that the group that returned with Ezra attempted to
restore the walls but this attempt was thwarted by the Samaritans (Ezra 4:11,12,23).
This attempt must have been under Ezra in 458 BC, because the decree granted him just
such extended powers (7:18, 25; 9:9).

(D) Artaxerxes 445 BC in his 20th year (Nehemiah 2). This gave Nehemiah permission to
rebuild the walls (Nehemiah2). Many believe this is the decree because it emphasises the
walls but as we have seen a previous attempt had been made on the basis of the earlier
decree. It was the failure to implement that decree that upset Nehemiah and he gained
permission to assist in accomplishing the work undertaken by Ezra which had been retarded.
So this was not the originating decree but a renewal of the earlier one.

Therefore Daniel's 70 Weeks start in 458 BC.

DANIEL'S 70 WEEKS
Daniel 9:24-27

1. THE PROPHECY

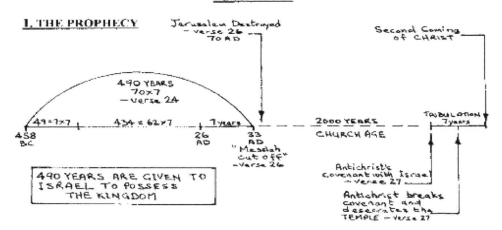

Jerusalem Destroyed
– verse 26
70 AD

Second Coming
of CHRIST

490 YEARS
70×7
– verse 24

49=7×7 | 434 = 62×7 | 7 years

458 BC

26 AD

33 AD
"Messiah
cut off"
– verse 26

2000 YEARS
CHURCH AGE

TRIBULATION
7 years

490 YEARS ARE GIVEN TO
ISRAEL TO POSSESS
THE KINGDOM

Antichrist's
covenant with Israel
– verse 27

Antichrist breaks
covenant and
desecrates the
TEMPLE – verse 27

2. GOD'S PLAN A

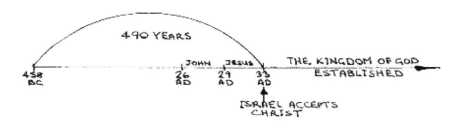

490 YEARS

JOHN | JESUS | THE KINGDOM OF GOD
ESTABLISHED

458 BC

26 AD

29 AD

33 AD

ISRAEL ACCEPTS
CHRIST

3. GOD'S PLAN B

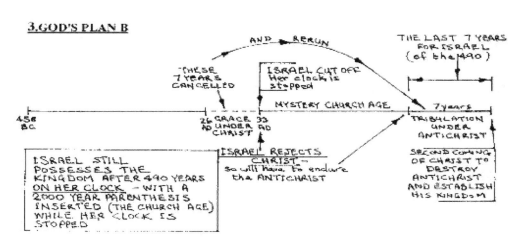

AND RERUN

THE LAST 7 YEARS
FOR ISRAEL
(of the 490)

THESE
7 YEARS
CANCELLED

ISRAEL CUT OFF
Her clock is
stopped

MYSTERY CHURCH AGE

7 years

458 BC

26 AD
GRACE
UNDER
CHRIST

33 AD

TRIBULATION
UNDER
ANTICHRIST

ISRAEL REJECTS
CHRIST –
so will have to endure
the ANTICHRIST

SECOND COMING
OF CHRIST TO
DESTROY
ANTICHRIST
AND ESTABLISH
HIS KINGDOM

ISRAEL STILL
POSSESSES THE
KINGDOM AFTER 490 YEARS
ON HER CLOCK – WITH A
2000 YEAR PARENTHESIS
INSERTED (THE CHURCH AGE)
WHILE HER CLOCK IS
STOPPED

Framework Prophecy 2

THE OLIVET DISCOURSE OF JESUS.

Jesus' great prophecy expounds and builds upon Daniel's 70 Weeks.

The theme of Matthew is Jesus presenting Himself as Israel's MESSIAH-KING, their rejection of Him and the results. This rejection came to a climax in chapter 12 with Jesus casting out a blind and dumb spirit - a MESSIANIC MIRACLE. Their deliberate rejection of Him despite such proof manifested in accusing Him of being able to do this because He was possessed by satan. He warned them of committing the unforgivable sin and told them He would only give them one more sign (chance to believe) - the sign of Jonah - His death and resurrection after 3 days (v39,16:1-4). In a parable where ISRAEL is a HOUSE, He warns them of the coming destruction if they reject Him and refuse to let Him in (v43-45) John cleaned up Israel, but if they reject Christ they will be empty and open for destruction and their last state (dispersion) will be worse than the first (occupation)

Chapter 21 Jesus' triumphal Entry - He presented Himself as their King but knew the leaders had rejected Him and so prophesied the resulting destruction coming on Jerusalem (Luke 19:41-44).

Chapter 23 He pronounced woes (judgements) on Israel's leaders for rejecting Him (see v37) concluding: **"Your house** (the Temple) **is left to you desolate...you will see me no more until you say. "Blessed is He** (Messiah) **who comes in the name of the Lord"** (v38,39). He was signifying that He was turning away from Israel until they receive him as their King.

Chapter 24: "Then Jesus went out and departed from the Temple" (24:1). This action signified the glory leaving the Temple prior to its destruction.

"His disciples came to Him to show Him the buildings of the Temple and Jesus said to them,"See all these things? Verily I say to you, there will not be left here one stone upon another, that shall not be thrown down"

(Matthew 24:1,2). This was literally fulfilled in AD 70 when the Romans destroyed Jerusalem. Despite Titus' wishes the Temple was burnt and the molten gold went between all the cracks of the stones so that by the time gold hunters had finished every stone was dismantled! So we see that Jesus is predicting judgement coming upon Israel for rejecting her Messiah.

Now the disciples ask 3 Questions

- the answers to which are the basis of Jesus' famous prophecy.

As well as in **Matthew 24**, it is in **Mark 13** and **Luke 21**
- we have to combine these three to get the full prophecy.
See the Appendix at the end for a detailed harmonisation.

Matthew 24:3 and Mark 13:4 give the three questions the prophecy answers.
"As he sat on the mount of Olives (looking at the Temple),
the disciples came to him privately, saying, "Tell us,

Question(1): WHEN shall these things (the destruction of the Temple) **be?
and what shall be the SIGN when all these things come to pass?**

and (2) What shall be the SIGN of Your Coming?
(the Coming of Christ marks the 'telos' = the final end of the age)

and (3) (the SIGN) **of the end** ('suntelia' = the consummation, the closing)
of the age?" (this is talking about the TRIBULATION). 'suntelia' does not mean the final end like 'telos' but a period of time in which things are brought to their conclusion.

The key word here is SIGN. When you travel somewhere you look for signs before your destination that grab your attention and tell you how close you are to your goal. It is important to know and see the signs of the times. (In Matthew 16:1-3, Jesus rebuked the Pharisees for failing to discern the signs of the times and thus missing out on what God was doing).

Question 1. They asked for the sign by which they would know the Temple would soon be destroyed.

Question 2. They asked for the signs that would happen before the Second Coming; these are the signs of the final end ('telos').

Question 3. They asked for the signs by which we would know that the Tribulation was drawing near. These are the signs of the approach of the end or consummation ('suntelia') of the age.

Jesus answered these three questions giving three sets of signs.

He answered Question 1 in Luke 21:20-24: "When YOU SEE Jerusalem surrounded by armies (this is the SIGN) **then know her desolation is nigh."** The answer to WHEN the Temple would be destroyed was that it would be in the disciples' generation (it was a judgment on that generation for rejecting Christ). The SIGN they were to look for was the very next time that Jerusalem would be surrounded by armies - then they would know that the destruction was about to happen. This happened when Rome besieged Jerusalem in AD 67. **"Then let them in Judaea flee to the mountains; and them in the midst of it depart out; and let not them in the countries enter it. For these be the days of vengeance** (on Israel for rejecting her Messiah)**, that all things written may be fulfilled"** (Jesus was providing for the protection of believers in the terrible times predicted by Daniel 9:26). But how can they escape with Jerusalem surrounded? Due to trouble at Rome, the army pulled back for a time. So most thought things were O.K, but all the Christians mindful of Jesus' warning, fled to safety in Pella in Jordan. Soon after the Romans returned and destroyed the city and the Temple in AD 70. **"But woe to them with child, and them who give suck, in those days! for there shall be great DISTRESS in the land, and wrath** (judgement) **upon this people and they will fall by the edge of the sword, and be led away captive into all nations and Jerusalem shall be trodden down of the Gentiles, until the times of the Gentiles be fulfilled."**

FULFILLED! Israel was indeed scattered to the nations, but the 'until' signifies that this will only be for a certain set time of Gentile domination. Therefore, when the Times of the Gentiles are fulfilled, Israel will return, be restored as a nation and regain control of Jerusalem. In fact this part of the prophecy has also been fulfilled in 1948 (the rebirth of the nation) and 1967 (the capture of all Jerusalem). This signifies that the Times of the Gentiles (Gentile domination over Israel) have been fulfilled and that we are now living in a new final phase of this age. Later in this prophecy, Jesus confirms that this restoration of Israel is the key sign of being in the last generation before the end.

Jesus answered Question 2 (the SIGNS of His Second Coming) in Matthew 24:7-31, where He gives the succession of events (in the Tribulation) leading to the Second Coming. The Tribulation is a unique period of time just before the Return of Christ, so all the special events of the Tribulation are the signs of the Second Coming. Thus, He gives the various signs by which people will know they are in the Tribulation. He describes its start, middle and end.

But first, in v4-6, Jesus gave the GENERAL CHARACTERISTICS OF THIS AGE, Jesus answered (their question): **"Take heed no man deceive you. For many shall come in my name, saying, I am Christ; and shall deceive many and you shall hear of wars and rumours of wars: see you are not troubled for all these things must come to pass, BUT THE END** ('telos') **IS NOT YET** (imminent).**"**

These are not signs of any of the three events the disciples asked about. In particular, they are not signs of the END (the Second Coming). That is, they are not indicators of being in the Tribulation. However all these features grow in intensity throughout the age and climax in the Tribulation.

Having given what are NOT the signs of the End, Jesus then gave what are the signs of the End - that is the characteristics of the Tribulation (v7-14).

The use of 'telos' in v6 is significant. It shows that Jesus is in the process of answering Question 2 which concerns the 'telos' or Second Coming (this is confirmed by the use of 'telos' in v13,14). I used to think that verses 7-14 are the answer to Question 3 because they are the description of the 'suntelia' (Tribulation). However signs are something that happen before an event. We see from v6 that Jesus is thinking of signs in this way, for the events of the Tribulation (v7-14), are the true signs of the End (Second Coming) in contrast to the general characteristics of this Age (v4-6). Thus; "**BUT THE END** ('telos') **IS NOT YET"** is the point where Jesus turns from what are not signs to are the real signs of the End.

Jesus now describes the START OF THE TRIBULATION (see v8). This is parallel to John's account of the start of the Tribulation in Revelation 6.

(1) CONFLICT and WAR ON A WORLD-WIDE SCALE.

"**FOR** nation shall rise against nation, and kingdom against kingdom" (v7). This is an expression referring not just to a local war but World-War. The Tribulation will start with world-wide conflict. This corresponds to the first two Horseman of the Apocalypse (Rev 6:1-4). SEAL 1 releases the Rider on the White Horse (antichrist) who goes forth to conquer and releasing World-War and bloodshed (SEAL 2 - the Rider on the Red Horse).

(2) "There shall be FAMINES" (v7).

This is the Rider on a Black Horse (Revelation 6:5,6 = SEAL 3).

(3) "Pestilences, and earthquakes, in divers places" (v7).

One in four are killed (over one billion people!). This is the Rider on the Pale horse (Revelation 6:7,8 = SEAL 4).

The SEALS in Revelation 6 reveal the massive scale of the destruction way beyond anything that has happened in the past. These things will happen suddenly and all together in such a way that previous catastrophes will seem minor in comparison.

"**All these** (sign-events) **are the BEGINNING OF SORROWS** (literally '**the BEGINNING of BIRTH PAINS')**"(v8). That is, they mark the BEGINNING of the TRIBULATION. 'BIRTH PAINS' was a technical term for the sufferings which would immediately precede a new age, the Age of Messiah. All these happen at the start of of the Tribulation and continue through the first half of the Tribulation. As birth-pains grow in intensity as the birth (of the Kingdom) approaches, so these disasters will intensify and get even worse in the second half of the Tribulation. This is the 'sudden destruction' of 1Thessalonians 5:2,3:

"You yourselves know perfectly that the Day of the Lord (the Tribulation) **so comes as a thief in the night. For when they say, "Peace and safety!" then sudden destruction comes upon them, as labour pains upon a pregnant woman and they shall not escape."**

(4) A great world-wide persecution of believers and Jews.
"Then shall they deliver you up to Tribulation, and shall kill you and you will be hated of all nations for my name's sake" (v9)   (Compare Rev6:9-11= SEAL 5). Jeremiah 30:7 calls it: **"The time of Jacob's Trouble."** It is pictured by the seven years of famine in the time of JOSEPH. It is a time of testing and sifting of unbelievers from believers, as sin comes to its fullness. **"Then shall many be offended, and betray one another, and hate one another and many false prophets shall rise, and shall deceive many and because iniquity shall abound, the love of many shall wax cold. But he** (the believer) **who endures** (in faith) **to the END** (of the Tribulation) **will be saved** (by Christ at His Return)" (v10-13).   v13 shows that these conditions will continue to the END ('telos') of the Tribulation when Christ returns. Again this confirms Jesus is answering Question 2. At the end Israel will receive and welcome Jesus as her Messiah-King.   He returns to deliver her from the Tribulation and through her establish His Kingdom.

(5) Signs in the Sky: "There will be fearful sights and great signs from heaven" (Luke 21:11). Compare Revelation 6:12-17 = SEAL 6.

(6) "This Gospel of the Kingdom shall be preached in all the world for a witness to all nations; and then shall the END come" (v14). There will be the world-wide preaching of the Gospel throughout the Tribulation. This great move of evangelism will be initiated by 144,000 anointed Jews and continued by their converts, not the Church (see Revelation 7), proclaiming again that the Messianic Kingdom is at hand - as John and Jesus preached in the first century. The recent Rapture will have awakened many to the reality of

Christ, making then open to the Gospel. The Harmony of the Olivet Discourse shows that Jesus also predicted the world-wide preaching of the gospel in the Church-age (Mark 13:10). The END is 'telos', the final end, the Return of Christ. Again, this shows that Jesus is answering Question 2. All these things (including evangelism) must happen and continue to the END of the Tribulation. v7-14 are the SIGNS that indicate the START of the Tribulation (v7). All of these things (including a new world-wide evangelistic outreach) will occur together near the start of the Tribulation and continue for seven years with increasing intensity. Next He gives the special signs for the MIDDLE and END of the Tribulation.

Next Jesus gives the SPECIFIC SIGN of being at MID-TRIBULATION:
"When you therefore shall SEE the Abomination of desolation, spoken of by Daniel the prophet, stand in the holy place" (v15).
This happens MID-TRIBULATION when the antichrist breaks his covenant with Israel and invades, setting up an idol of himself in the Temple (see Daniel 9:27).
"Whoso READS, let him understand" (v15 - compare Daniel 9:25).
'Reads' indicates that this will happen in a later generation. This is similar to what happened in the first century. In both cases the Roman Ruler comes to take Jerusalem. This is a sign to believers to flee immediately. There is then three and a half years of mounting trouble and destruction for Israel until the end but the believers are kept safe (Revelation 12:6). So, still answering Question 2, Jesus gives the sign of antichrist's Abomination of Desolation which tells us when Christ's Coming (the end) is three and a half years away.

This statement by Jesus gives confirmation of our interpretation of Daniel's 70 Weeks:
(1) Jesus was looking for a literal fulfilment of an event in the 70th Week, showing we should take the whole prophecy literally, including the timing.
(2) The fact that this event was still future to Jesus confirms that Daniel meant 70 Weeks (Sevens) of years not days. **(3)** Jesus still expected the prophecy of the 70th Week to be fulfilled in the future even though He knew He was already at the end of the 70th Week. This means He understood that there was a postponement of the fulfilment of the 70th Week because of Israel's sin. He had come to Israel exactly when Daniel had predicted but was not able to establish the Kingdom at that time because Israel rejected Him. However, Daniel's prophecy anticipated such a delay was possible.

"Then (when you see the Abomination) **let them in Judaea flee to the mountains** (this prophecy is the key to the preservation of the believers in Israel at this time). **Let him on the housetop not come down to take anything out of his house. Neither let him in the field return to take his clothes and woe to them with child, and those giving suck in those days! But pray that your flight be not in the winter or sabbath day. For then will be GREAT TRIBULATION, such as was not since the beginning of the world to this time, no, nor ever shall be. Except those days should be shortened, there would be no flesh saved: but for the elect's sake those days shall be shortened"** (v16-22).

This marks the start of the second half of the Tribulation - called the GREAT TRIBULATION (it is far worse than the first half).
It will come to a climax at the Battle of Armageddon where if Jesus did not intervene all mankind would be destroyed. But Jesus comes to deliver believing Israel who are calling on Him to return as their King and save them. The days are shortened by the personal Return of the Lord to save believing Israel.

Notice that although Jesus predicted Israel would be scattered to the nations in Luke21:24, He also is saying they will be back as a nation in the land by the time the Tribulation starts, for the prophecies of the Tribulation assume this.

Still answering Question 2, Jesus now gives the SIGN indicating the END of the Tribulation - the final sign just before His Second Coming (Matthew 24:23-30).

First, He describes counterfeit signs of His Return, which are to be rejected and not to be acted upon. He says it is not a quiet or secret Coming that requires someone to tell you that it has happened:

"Then (in the Great Tribulation) **if any man says to you, 'Lo, here is Christ, or there'; believe it not. For there will arise false Christs, and false prophets, and shall show great signs and wonders** (especially antichrist) **so that, if it were possible, they will deceive the very elect** (believing Jews). **Behold, I have told you before. So if they say to you, 'Behold,**

He is in the desert', go not forth (out of their place of hiding and safety)
'behold, He is in the secret chambers', believe it not" (v23-26).

Next he gives the true and unmistakable SIGN of His Coming:
"For as the LIGHTNING comes out of the east, and shines even to the
west; so shall also the Coming of the Son of man be."
(It will be visible to all, nobody will have to tell you as in v23-26).
Where and when?   "For wherever the carcass is, there the vultures
will be gathered together" (v27,28). It will be when the armies of the world
gather at the Battle of Armageddon to destroy Israel.   Christ will return to where
the vultures (the invading nations, inspired by satan) have all gathered to eat
the carcass of Israel, for He will come to destroy them and deliver Israel.
Thus a sign of being within weeks or days from the end is the gathering at
Megiddo of a massive multinational force to invade and destroy Israel.

"Immediately after the TRIBULATION of those days shall the sun be
darkened and the moon shall not give her light and the stars shall
fall from heaven and the powers of the heavens shall be shaken."
Just before it happens there will be a worldwide Blackout for a day -
see Zechariah 14:6 - and other cosmic upheavals.
This is the sign of being in the last few hours before the end.

"And then shall APPEAR (shine forth) the SIGN of the Son of Man
in heaven and then shall all the tribes of the earth mourn."
The appearance of His Glory is the Sign that come immediately before His
personal appearance.   Because of the Blackout, only His glory will be seen
in that day. "and they shall (all together) SEE the Son of Man coming
in the clouds of heaven with power and great glory" (v29-30).
It will be so majestic everyone on earth will see it together.

"And He shall send forth his angels with a great sound of a Trumpet and
they shall gather together his elect (Israel) from the four winds, from one
end of heaven to another" (v31). The final regathering of Israel will be at

Christ's Second Coming. Jesus stays with this thought as He gives the general sign of being near the Tribulation - the Fig-Tree (v32-33) - the initial regathering of Israel (in unbelief) which is fulfilled in our time.   This is the sign of being in the generation immediately before the end.

We have seen that Jesus confirmed and built upon the revelation of the prophets; especially we see how Jesus' prophecy connects with and builds on Daniel's prophecy as He interprets it literally.

Jesus then answered Question 3: **"What is the SIGN of the end of the age?"** Or: how can we know if we are in the time just before the Tribulation? His subject is the Tribulation, the Day of the Lord, and what will happen just before it. This question is, how can we know that we are in the time just before the Tribulation?   What are the signs?   We shall see that the signs given by Jesus are the SIGNS OF OUR TIMES. These signs tell us that we are now living in this special time - the last days of the Church Age! By harmonising Luke 21:28-36, Matthew 24:32-44 and Mark 13:28-37, we can get an idea of Jesus' full answer as to which signs precede the Tribulation. This passage us great relevance to us today. Notice that the removal of believers immediately before this Day begins is a major theme.

Luke 21:28-33: **"Now <u>when these things begin to happen, look up and lift up your heads, because your redemption draws near</u>. Then He spoke to them a Parable: "Look at the Fig Tree, and all the trees. When they are already budding, you see and know for yourselves that Summer is now near. So you also, when you see these things happening, know that the Kingdom of God is near. Assuredly, I say to you, this generation will by no means pass away till all things take place. Heaven and earth will pass away, but My words will by no means pass away."**

Matthew 24:36-42: **"But of that day and hour no one knows, not even the angels of heaven, but My Father only. But as the days of Noah were, so also will the Coming of the Son of Man be. For as in the days before the flood, they were eating and drinking, marrying and giving in marriage, <u>until the day that Noah entered the ark, and did not know until the flood came and took them all away,</u>**

so also will the Coming of the Son of Man be. Then two men will be in the field: one will be taken and the other left. Two women will be grinding at the mill: one will be taken and the other left. Watch therefore, for you do not know what hour your Lord is coming."

Luke 21:34-36: "But take heed to yourselves, lest your hearts be weighed down with carousing, drunkenness, and cares of this life, and that Day come on you unexpectedly. For it will come as a snare on all those who dwell on the face of the whole earth. Watch therefore, and pray always that you may be counted worthy to escape all these things that will come to pass, and to stand before the Son of Man."

Mark 13:34-37: "It is like a man going to a far country, who left his house and gave authority to his servants, and to each his work, and commanded the doorkeeper to watch. Watch therefore, for you do not know when the master of the house is coming - in the evening, at midnight, at the crowing of the rooster, or in the morning - lest, coming suddenly, he find you sleeping. And what I say to you, I say to all: Watch!"

Matthew 24:43-44: "But know this, that if the master of the house had known what hour the thief would come, he would have watched and not allowed his house to be broken into. Therefore you also be ready, for the Son of Man is coming at an hour you don't expect."

His answer contains three main signs:

(1) The FIG-TREE = The Rebirth of the Nation of Israel.

(2) 'All the TREES' = 'All these things' (of which the Fig-Tree is the most prominent) are the various characteristics of the Tribulation, the signs of the end that Jesus has just described. These signs are described as Trees because they grow. Thus although they only reach maturity in the Tribulation, they must must appear and be growing before the Tribulation. So the time before the Tribulation is marked by the appearance of ALL these things together and growing in intensity. The signs of the Tribulation will be 'these Trees' springing up, followed by the Rapture.

(3) The RAPTURE, the escape or disappearance of believers is the final sign that happens immediately before the Tribulation begins.

Jesus introduces this new section by saying: **"Now when <u>these things</u>** (the world-conditions and events of the Tribulation that Jesus had just described in answering Question 2) **begin to happen, look up and lift up your heads because your redemption** (the Rapture) **draws near "** (Luke 21:28).

He goes back in time before the Tribulation begins, in order to answer Question 3. He is saying: *"when you see <u>the beginnings of these things,</u> then you know the Tribulation is soon approaching."*
He is pointing to the origin of 'these things' in the time just before the Tribulation starts. The 'beginning of these things' speak of a special period of time that closes the Church Age and leads up to the Tribulation.

To find when this time-period starts we need to look back at the previous verses in Luke. v25-27 show how 'these things' end in the Second Coming of Christ, but v24 tells us how we can know that this time has begun:

"They (Israel) **will fall by the edge of the sword, and be led away captive into all nations. And Jerusalem will be trampled by Gentiles <u>until the Times of the Gentiles are fulfilled</u>."**

It is <u>the ending of the Times of the Gentiles and the consequent restoration of Israel to the Land (1948) and the recapture of Jerusalem (1967) that clearly shows that we are in time of the beginning of 'these things'</u>, a new phase of history, the final build-up for the Tribulation. The direct consequence of the ending of the Times of the Gentiles (that Jesus points out here) is the rebirth of Israel and the recapture of Jerusalem. This provides a confirmation, because 'these things' that must be fulfilled in the end-time must include the restoration of Israel (the Fig-Tree, v29-31). The time just before the Tribulation is characterised by the Fig-Tree (Israel), and its reappearance requires the ending of the Times of the Gentiles. So, the final phase of the Church-Age began when the Times of the Gentiles were fulfilled (we shall study this more in Part 3).

Thus a key marker of being in this new time-period is Israel and so we entered this final phase at or before 1948. We shall see that the Times of the Gentiles began to wind down from 1914, which is perhaps when these new final phase of this age began.

Luke 21:24 divides the Church-Age into three parts: (1) The first generation - the time up to the destruction of Jerusalem and the scattering of Israel to the nations, (2) An extended period of time with Israel out of the land, under Gentile domination, (3) A final generation that sees the restoration of Israel and recapture of Jerusalem at the close of the Times of the Gentiles.

In conclusion, Luke 21:24 gives the starting point for 'these things' that characterise the closing of the age, 'the last of the last days'. Then v25-27 describe how 'these things' will come to an end. v28 says that when you see these things begin, in particular Israel's rebirth and possession of Jerusalem (v24), then get ready for you know the Rapture is near! Then v29-32 says that the total time-period from when we see 'these things' start happening until they are all fulfilled at the Second Coming is within a man's lifespan. Thus the total length of this final period of time must be 120 years or less.

Luke concludes this Section: **"But take heed to yourselves, lest... that Day** (the Tribulation) **come on you unexpectedly. For it will come as a snare** (a trap that will suddenly snap tight) **on all those who dwell on the face of the whole earth. Watch therefore, and pray always that you may be counted worthy to <u>escape all these things</u>** (the troubles of the Tribulation) **that will come to pass, and to stand** (resurrected) **before the Son of Man** (in the Rapture)" (v34-36). This confirms that Jesus has gone back to the time before the Tribulation and promises there will be an escape from the 'Tribulation trap', provided for believers just before the Tribulation events ('all these things') come to pass. This is as plain a statement as you could wish for, of a Pre-Tribulational Rapture! Jesus gives the major SIGN (Tree) by which we can know we are in the final generation- the time just before the Tribulation,in the parable of the Fig-Tree.

SIGN (1): THE FIG-TREE

"Now learn the Parable of the FIG TREE: when its branch has already become tender and puts forth leaves, you know that Summer is near. So you also, when you see all these things, know that it (the Kingdom) is near - at the doors!   Assuredly, I say to you, this generation will by no means pass away till all these things take place" (Matthew 24:32-34).

It is clear that the first thing to look for is the FIG TREE, but what is it? The Fig-Tree in the Bible represents ISRAEL.   Jeremiah 24 shows Israel in captivity as a basket of figs. This is because they are no longer a Fig-Tree planted in the Land but scattered). See also Hosea 9:10, Joel 1:6,7; Ezekiel 36:8. The Fig-Tree as Israel is confirmed by Jesus' use of this symbol in Luke 13:6-9.   Thus the major sign of being in the end-times, just before the Tribulation is the reappearance of Israel as a living nation.

Jesus had started this Parable of the Fig Tree earlier.

He is now bringing it to its conclusion. This parable is therefore in two parts:

(1) Jesus came to the Fig-Tree (Israel) to inspect its fruit (faith) and found none so he announced that he will cut it down and remove it from the land (Luke 13:1-9).   He symbolically acted this out when He cursed a Fig-Tree and it withered from its roots (Mark 11:12-24, Matthew 21:18-19). The judgment started immediately (but invisibly - at the roots, the trees' source of life) but was only visibly manifested some time later ('the next day'). This was fulfilled in AD33 when Israel was cut off spiritually, and then in AD70 this judgment was manifested when Israel was expelled from the land.

(2) But Jesus also predicted that the Fig-Tree will rise again!:
"Learn the parable of the FIG TREE (ISRAEL), when his branch is become tender, and puts forth leaves (not fruit) you know SUMMER (the Millennial Kingdom) is nigh" (Matthew 24:32).

So, the Fig-tree is Israel which was cut down and cursed by Christ for rejecting her Messiah. But she will spring up again and then we can know that Summer

(the Kingdom) is near. Luke confirms this: **"Look at the Fig Tree, and all the trees. When they are already budding, you see and know for yourselves that Summer is now near.   So you also, when you see these things happening, know that the Kingdom of God is near"** (Luke 21:29-31).
Luke makes it clear that Summer represents the Messianic Kingdom.

The sign of being in the final generation before the Kingdom is the Fig-Tree with its leaves shooting forth, for all to see.   All of history is moving towards the Kingdom (Summer) when Israel (the Fig-Tree) will bear mature fruit. In the Tribulation, especially by the end, as Summer approaches, this fruit (faith) will start to appear.   In the Spring (the season before Summer) the Tree grows and puts forth leaves and these are signs that Summer is soon to come.   So Jesus is saying that the sign of being in the time-season just before the end of the age is the reappearance of Israel on the world-scene.

The Fig-Tree is now putting forth its leaves for all to see. The Rebirth of Israel (1948) and her further growth (1967) is the clear-cut sign that we are in the last days of the Church Age! The Fig-Tree has reappeared and put forth leaves (but not fruit) as Jesus predicted! This confirms other prophecies that Israel as a nation will first of all be regathered to the land in unbelief (leaves only) and will only come to faith in Christ (bear fruit) later.

Next, Jesus went even further saying that Israel was God's Time Clock.
The Rebirth of Israel would start the final countdown:
"Verily I say to you, this generation (that sees the Fig-Tree) **shall not pass away, until ALL THESE THINGS be fulfilled"** (Luke 21:32).

The generation who see this amazing Sign of the Fig-Tree (those alive to see the events of 1948) will not all die (pass away) before all the events of the Tribulation and Second Coming are fulfilled.
Jesus reinforced this amazing claim with great emphasis on its truth:
"Heaven and earth shall pass away, but my words shall not pass away" (v33). The Clock started at Israel's Rebirth and runs for a man's lifetime.

Thus we can see the SIGN OF THE FIG-TREE and KNOW that we are IN THE LAST GENERATION. As Israel gets older and puts forth leaves, she is a sure sign of the imminent start of the Tribulation (the short transition into the Millennial Summer) when she will increasingly bear fruit.

The Fig-Tree gives the general, but not the exact time of Christ's Coming.

THE SIGN OF THE FIG-TREE

Jesus said: **"The generation that sees the Fig-Tree** (the nation of Israel) **put forth her leaves shall not all pass away before the end shall come."** Israel was reborn in the land in 1948, and began putting forth her leaves for all to see!

Out of the labour-pains of the World-Wars and Holocaust came the rebirth of the nation of Israel - the major miracle of this century. A nation dispersed to the nations regathered in her land once again as an independent nation after 2000 years. This is unheard of in all history! Moreover it was predicted by the prophets and by Jesus (Luke 21:24). The fact that Jesus gave the restored Fig-Tree as the key sign for the last generation is appropriate because the end-time prophecies require Israel to be restored to the land before the start of the Tribulation, and for Israel to be centre-stage again and in control of Jerusalem, with a rebuilt Temple (Daniel 9:27, Matthew 24:15-20). The stage has to be set before the final scene (the Tribulation) begins. Bible Prophecy of the nations is all centred on Israel and the Land, so we should expect this miraculous event to be a major end-time sign.

In Luke 21:20-24, in a prophecy outlining future events resulting from Israel's rejection of Jesus, He predicted the scattering of Israel among the nations in AD 70: **"And they will fall by the edge of the sword, and be led away captive into all nations. And Jerusalem will be trampled by Gentiles until the Times of the Gentiles are fulfilled."** (v24) This implies that a major marker of the time before the end is the regathering of Israel. (She must be back for the stage to be set for all the end-time prophecies of the Tribulation to be fulfilled). When Israel is back, the end comes soon after (v25-28). He confirms this in the PARABLE OF THE FIG-TREE (v29-33). This sign of the rebirth of the nation of Israel concerns the beginning of their regathering (the tree planted in the land beginning to put forth leaves tells us we are in the last generation), it does not require the regathering of Israel to be complete which only happens at the Second Coming. Matthew 24:31 describes the completion of the regathering, then in v32-34, Jesus said that when we see the regathering begin we know are in the last generation!

One aspect of the Fig-Tree's restoration is that full control of Jerusalem must be restored to Israel (Luke 21:24). In the Tribulation there will be a rebuilt and functioning Jewish Temple (Daniel 9:27, Matthew24:15; 2 Thessalonians 2:3,4; Revelation 11:1-2).   This requires prior Jewish control of the Temple area and therefore of Jerusalem so that it can be built (fulfilled in 1967).

THE VEIL OVER ISRAEL is removed in the Tribulation (144,000 Jewish evangelists will be anointed at the start). We would expect growing Jewish interest in Jesus and conversions in the time running up to this as a preparation for a great national turning to Christ. Today, there is a move of God among the Jews with increasing numbers turning to their Messiah.

SIGN (2): 'ALL THE TREES.'

The Parable of the Fig-Tree tells us about other signs that confirm that the Tribulation is near. **"Now when these things begin to happen, look up and lift up your heads, because your redemption draws near. Look at the FIG TREE, and ALL THE TREES. When they are already budding** (leaves), **you see and know for yourselves that Summer is now near. So you also, when you see these things happening, know that the Kingdom of God is near. Assuredly, I say to you, this generation will by no means pass away till all these things take place"** (Luke 21:28-32).

<u>Matthew says</u>: **"when you see ALL THESE THINGS, know that it is near, even at the doors"** (v33).   'All these things' must refer to the conditions of the Tribulation, mentioned just before by Jesus.

This says that as well as the sign of the Fig-Tree there are other signs (trees) indicating the closeness of the Tribulation. These are world-conditions that come to their fullness in the Tribulation.   Jesus had just mentioned some of these in His description of the Tribulation,and so they are also called 'these things' in v28,31). The Fig-Tree is the major sign for the approach of the Tribulation and 'all the Trees' are the other signs of the Tribulation. We know that Israel (the Fig-Tree) must be back in the land for the Tribulation. So her regathering must take place before this, and it is a sign that this time is approaching. The main sign is the Fig-Tree and the other signs (conditions and characteristics of the Tribulation) are represented by the other Trees.

Jesus uses trees to describe these kind of signs because they are not just one-off events but developing, maturing world-conditions. These Trees are full grown in the Tribulation.   He is telling us to look at the Trees (world-conditions) that are mature in the Tribulation. The time just before the Tribulation will be characterised, not just by the springing up of the Fig-Tree but of <u>ALL the Trees</u>. Moreover, the more these Trees develop and start budding (the more they resemble their final state in the Tribulation) the closer we must be to the

Tribulation. Just as Summer's approach is signalled by all the trees putting forth their leaves in Spring, so when we see all the world-conditions moving toward the Bible's description of the Tribulation we know we are close. Some of these trees are manifestations of evil forces that have been working and growing throughout the age but are only allowed to come to fullness in the Tribulation when their evil fruit will be ripe for the judgment that Christ executes at the end of the Tribulation, cutting down all trees that are not of Him (Matthew 3:7-1). The time just before the Tribulation is a special time when all the Trees put forth their leaves (they all develop and grow quickly into greater prominence and manifestation than before). We will look at the various Trees described by the Bible and observe how this is uniquely true of the present time.

All these Trees will start appearing in the time just before the Tribulation (like the Fig-Tree) or at least coming into greater visibility. Therefore if you see ALL of these Trees (signs) sprouting up together, you know that time is short. Moreover, as you see how all these trees are coming into fuller and greater manifestation (as the trees put forth leaves as Summer approaches), we can get a general idea of how close we are to the Tribulation. They are only full grown in the Tribulation (for example Israel will probably only have her Temple rebuilt and functioning in the Tribulation) but the closer we get, we will see each Tree get greater and more like the way it will be in the Tribulation. As we consider these other Trees now, you can judge to what degree things at the present time line up with what the Bible tells us world conditions will be at the end (in the Tribulation).

These Trees could be called Continuity Signs. Most prophecy jumps over the Church-Age and shows us the climax of history in the Tribulation. But the general world-conditions in the Tribulation can't just spring up overnight - they have to be present and growing before the Tribulation. All history is moving toward the climax of the Tribulation and so we can measure how close we are by how close general conditions are compared to what is going to be in the Tribulation. Certain conditions must be in place before the Tribulation begins. When we see these all happen together, we have strong evidence of being in the last generation. **"Now when** (all) **these things** (that will come to fullness in the

Tribulation) **begin to happen** (in the time just before the Tribulation), **look up and lift up your heads, because your redemption** (the Rapture) **draws near** " (Luke 21:28).   He is saying 'get ready', for the Tribulation is soon to start, but there will be a Rapture for believers first.

WHAT ARE SOME OF THESE TREES (signs of the Tribulation)?

1. THE BIRTH-PANGS   Jesus described the Tribulation as characterised by World-War, famine, disease, and earthquakes in the natural world; and worldwide anti-semitism, persecution of believers, apostasy, godlessness, lawlessness, as well as the rise of great religious deceptions in the form of many false prophets, cults and religions in the spiritual realm (Matthew 24:7-12). He called all these BIRTH PAINS - they are the signs of being in the last stages of a pregnancy: **"For nation shall rise against nation, and Kingdom against Kingdom** (world-wide conflict).   **There will be famines, pestilences** (diseases), **and earthquakes, in divers places** (world-wide).   **All these are the beginning of birth-pains** (the sorrows of the first-half of the Tribulation, that will intensify in the second-half or Great-Tribulation)" (Matthew 24:7,8).

As in a pregnancy, the birth pains of the Tribulation will come on suddenly, and increase in intensity as the Birth approaches (see the Book of Revelation). These will indicate that the end is very soon. However, these pains exist in a measure throughout the age (v4-6). As in a pregnancy, we expect the discomfort to increase. The baby (the Kingdom of God on earth) is GROWING invisibly. Its birth is at a set time. As it grows and the time gets closer to its birth, the conflict also increases within the mother (the present world-order) until it reaches a climax in the final pains (the Tribulation). The baby (the new world-order) has to overcome resistance within the mother just before being manifested, which sets up the labour-pains. But just before these final pains, women also have Braxton-Hicks contractions, premature (false) labour pains, which feel just like labour pains, but the birth is not yet immediate. However, they do indicate that the time of labour-pains is approaching quickly. This is the time we are in now, just before the final pains of the Tribulation begin.

131

Thus the time just before the Tribulation should be marked by a steady increase in MASSIVE WORLDWIDE WARFARE among the nations, EARTHQUAKES, FAMINES, DISEASES, and other disturbances of nature; anti-semitism, persecutions and many deceptions in the religious world and godlessness and lawlessness in society.

World War and natural disasters. The 20th Century certainly fulfilled this criteria in a unique way with World Wars 1 and 2 (in previous centuries World-War was impossible). In fact, 1914 marks the start of this final phase of history. Since then we have also seen an exponential increase of earthquakes, disease, persecutions, famines and false religion around the world. This shows that we are getting very close to the final (and even worse) pains of the Tribulation. (Many thought they were in the Tribulation in World War 2 with good reason because of the birth-pain prophecy, but it couldn't have been so, because it is also necessary for Israel to be back).

"THE 11th HOUR" In the World-Wars God gave us a sign that the end of the age is near. The Lord's Return is described as being at the MIDNIGHT hour: **"At MIDNIGHT there was a cry made, Behold the Bridegroom comes"** (Matthew 25:6). God clearly marked 11 o'clock when WORLD WAR 1 ended on: **The 11th hour of the 11th day of the 11th month** of 1918 exactly **11 months** after General Allenby entered Jerusalem and freed it from Turkish domination (11th December 1917) - a major step to Israel's rebirth - for at that time Britain committed to make it a homeland for the Jews.

WORLD-WAR and the RESTORATION of ISRAEL are two key signs of being in the last days before the Lord's Return (Matthew 24). Both began to occur together and marked the start of the FINAL HOUR of the Age (11pm), confirmed by God in the timing of the end of World War 1.

INCREASING EVIL The Book of Revelation shows great evil during the Tribulation. Moral conditions don't just suddenly change so there must be a great decline in morality before the Tribulation to prepare the way for the final manifestation of evil (so that God may judge it). Paul predicts this increase of evil in the last days of the Church Age: **"Know this, that in the last (of the last) days perilous times will come: For men will be lovers of themselves, lovers of money, boasters, proud, blasphemers, disobedient to parents, unthankful, unholy, unloving, unforgiving, slanderers, without self-control, brutal, despisers of good, traitors, headstrong, haughty, lovers of pleasure rather than lovers of God, having a form of godliness but denying its power. And from such people turn away!"** (2 Timothy 3:1-5). This describes our times very well.

APOSTASY. The Bible also predicts the growth of apostasy (falling away) from Biblical faith within the Church, towards the last days of the Church Age:

"Now the Spirit expressly says that in latter times some will depart from the faith, giving heed to deceiving spirits and doctrines of demons, speaking lies in hypocrisy, having their own conscience seared with a hot iron, forbidding to marry, and commanding to abstain from foods which God created to be received with thanksgiving by those who believe and know the truth" (1Timothy 4:1-3).

See also Matthew 13 and 2Peter 3:3-9. This apostasy will reaches a climax in the Tribulation in Mystery Babylon (Revelation 17) - a world-wide 'harlot' church. Again this requires the time just before the Tribulation to see a great increase in apostasy and the beginnings of the formation of a unified apostate church. This has certainly happened over the last 100 years.

ANTICHRIST. The ultimate incarnation of evil, a devil-possessed man will be revealed and come to power in the Tribulation. For a short time he will head a One-World Government, Economy and Religion. This final manifestation is presently being held back by the Church (2Thess 2:3-8), but the spirit of antichrist has been at work in the Church-Age (v7). So the full manifestation of antichrist is in the Tribulation but it is even now working in the world (1John 4:3).

Thus it is increasing and growing as we approach the end until it manifests in the antichrist himself. Thus its increased activity is a sign of being in the last times: **"as ye have heard that antichrist shall come, even now are there many antichrists; whereby we know that it is the last time"** (1John 2:18). The spirit of antichrist denies faith in God and Jesus Christ (1John 2:22, 4:3; 2John 1:7) and instead declares the divinity of man and his evolutionary rise to godhood. Thus, the unprecedented growth of New Age religion, atheism, evolution and secular humanism in recent times is another sign of the end - as Peter predicted: **"Knowing this first: that scoffers will come in the last days, walking according to their own lusts, and saying, "Where is the promise of His Coming? For since the fathers fell asleep, all things continue as they were from the beginning of creation"** (2Peter 3:3,4).

The ultimate aim of this satanic spirit is to displace God and Christ from human affairs. Thus it is working towards establishing a One-World Government, Economy and Religion ruled over by the antichrist.

One-World Religion: At Mid-Tribulation antichrist destroys the harlot church in order to replace it with a One-World Religion centred on the worship of man as god and the worship of antichrist himself as the supreme god, supported by satanic miracles. Thus in the end-time we would expect to see the rise of inter-faith, one-world religious movements, which in the name of unity, downplay the emphasis on an objective Creator God and His revelation, and replace this it by subjective seeking after 'spiritual forces' and experiencing the 'divine' power within. This New Age religion developing today is occultic. Different religions are seen as offering equally valid subjective ways to experience the 'divine'.

A One-World Government and Economy will also be set up at Mid-Tribulation. This means that the time just before the Tribulation will see great forces of Globalisation at work along with rapid advances in communications and technology to make this possible. Again this is uniquely true about our time in history. Global economic and political forces are eating away at national sovereignty, preparing the way for a One-World Order. The UN and IMF are manifestations of these forces at work. After World War 1, mankind started to rebuild the Tower of Babel (for the first time in 4500 years). God will let it reach its full proud height before sending it crashing down.

2. The POLITICS leading up to the Tribulation (Part 3 has more on this).

Israel and the Middle-East. Prophecy requires Israel to be back in the land before the Tribulation and to become central to world affairs. The final battle is over Israel. The Tribulation starts with antichrist making a peace treaty with Israel, so there must be Middle-East tension requiring a 'saviour' there.

Europe: The Tribulation sees a Revived Roman (European) Empire headed by the antichrist making a final bid to establish a One World Government (see Daniel and Revelation). These situations can't just appear - their seeds must be growing in the years just before the Tribulation. We certainly see great forces at work to form a Federated European Union, the heart of a Revived Roman Empire. The developing governmental structure of the EU is well-described by the feet (10 toes) of iron and clay (Dan 2), the form of Rome in the Tribulation before antichrist becomes absolute dictator at Mid-Tribulation. There has not been a European Political Unit since the Roman Empire.

A clear sign of the end-times is that we see one forming today! The end-time Revived Roman Empire is developing before our eyes as prophecy predicts.

Russia: Political conditions must also line up (which they do) for the Russian invasion of Israel in Ezekiel 38,39, which probably takes place before the Tribulation. It pictures her as a large, powerful country, invading Israel for spoil. See Book 3 for more details of this invasion.

3. The Tribulation is a time of ADVANCED SCIENCE (which tells us that the years leading up to it are ones of great scientific progress)

- INCREASE IN KNOWLEDGE and **WORLDWIDE TRAVEL** (Daniel 12:1,4)

- WORLDWIDE T.V: the broadcast of the death and resurrection of the two witnesses will be seen across the whole world at one time (Revelation 11:7-12).

- THE MARK of the BEAST (Revelation 13:16-18) is a means of controlling the masses, whereby people receive an identifying mark in their body which allows them to buy and sell. Only recent computer technology makes such a system possible. With implanted computer chips 'big-brother government could oversee and control all buying and selling in a cashless society, as well as knowing where everyone is.

The world with advancing technology, is moving towards registering every person with a number, so that Government can have complete records including all financial transactions. Plans are being laid for a global economic framework and for the use of standardised Smart Cards with computer chips to facilitate and record financial transfers. Biometric identification technologies have now been developed which can scan fingerprint, face or retina and convert the data into a number for identification. Many good justifications will be given for each new level but they are all steps toward preparing society psychologically and technologically for the ultimate system which will integrate all of these into one standardised and unified system of global control - the mark of the beast. To be part of this system one will have to deny the true God and give all allegiance to the State and its leader, but most will do it because without the mark and your number, you will be excluded from society and under the threat of death if captured (for treason).

- THE IMAGE of the BEAST (Revelation 13:14,15) seems to have life and be able to speak and interact with people. This could involve advanced virtual-reality computer technology.

- WEAPONS of MASS- DESTRUCTION Mankind is about to destroy itself when Jesus returns (Matthew24:21,22). Therefore man must first develop nuclear weapons and the capacity to wage World-War (only true since 1945).

- TRAVEL and COMMUNICATIONS allow world-wide preaching of the Gospel in the Tribulation (Matthew 24:14).

To prepare the way for all this, the century before the Tribulation must see a great increase in TECHNOLOGY. <u>Clearly this is uniquely true about the last 100 years</u> - with computers, planes, etc.

4. "<u>LIKE THE DAYS OF NOAH</u>"   More signs to recognise the near approach of the Tribulation can be deduced from the fact that Jesus compared the last days to the time of Noah: **"<u>As the days of Noah, so shall also the Coming of the Son of man be.</u>   For <u>as in the days before the flood</u> they were eating and drinking, marrying and giving in marriage, until the day that Noah entered into the Ark, and knew not until the flood came, and took them all away; <u>so shall also the Coming of the Son of man be</u>"** (Matthew 24:37-39).

This passage is part of His answer to Question 3, and so He is describing the time before the Tribulation.   Noah's Flood is a type of the Tribulation. Both are times of world-wide judgment (Matt 24:39; Luke 21:35).   The days before the Flood of Tribulation judgments fall upon the whole world, will be like the days of Noah before the Flood of God's judgment was poured out upon all flesh. Therefore we would expect the special characteristics of Noah's time will be repeated before the Tribulation.

The days of Noah were marked by:
1. MUCH OCCULT ACTIVITY and ILLICIT SEX (Genesis 6:2,4).
The strict barriers God set between humans and angels were broken, resulting in massive demonic infiltration of humanity in Noah's time. The satanic control and miracles of antichrist probably means that in the days of his birth and growth occultism is used widely and is well-developed on the earth. We see this clearly in our time with the mushrooming interest in these things in the last 40 years.

2. GREAT WICKEDNESS, CORRUPTION and VIOLENCE everywhere - a major decline of all moral standards (Genesis 6:5,11,12).

3. MATERIALISM and GODLESSNESS (Matthew 24:38).   The 120 years in which Noah was preparing the Ark were marked by steadily deteriorating moral conditions with society forgetting God and pursuing natural things.

4. HOMOSEXUALITY. A similar passage compares the last days to the days of Lot (Luke 17:28-32) in Sodom and Gommorrah - again marked by the throwing off of all moral restraint, resulting in the growth of violence and open HOMOSEXUALITY. Again this is characteristic of our times.

5. A POPULATION EXPLOSION (Genesis 6:1) - this happened during the 20th Century in an unprecedented way. There must be a huge world population in the Tribulation for there is a single army of 200 million (Revelation 9:16). Thus, the time just before it must see great population growth as Jesus predicted. This has uniquely been true of the last 100 years.

6. SCIENCE The time of Noah was a time of great SCIENTIFIC PROGRESS, as evidenced by the building of the Ark. We have only made ships that big in the recently. The last 100 years have been unique in rapid scientific progress. **It is evident our days parallel the days of Noah!**

THE GOSPEL Noah was able to preach the Gospel to the whole world (Hebrews 11:7; 2Peter 2:5). His massive Ark would have aroused great curiosity and everyone would have heard of and gone to see it. Noah preached to them the coming judgment and the Good-News of the salvation God offered if they believed His word. Likewise by the end of the Church-Age the Gospel of salvation from judgment (including those of the Tribulation) must be preached to all nations (Mark 13:10) in fulfilment of the Great Commission (Matthew 28:18-20, Mark 16:15). In Revelation 5:9 the raptured Church in Heaven consists of people from every people-group. As the whole world before the Flood could hear the Gospel, so the whole world before the Tribulation likewise. This is happening in our times as never before.

By mentioning all the trees with the Fig-Tree as signs operating even before the Tribulation, Jesus is confirming that the birth-pangs of the Tribulation will be experienced to a degree in the special time (100 years or so) just before the Tribulation and so are signs that the Tribulation is close. It is interesting that Jesus compared the end-time to Noah's time when there was a special period of 120 years (Genesis 6:3) which was the final build-up to the flood, during which

Noah preached and got the word out to all those living on the earth that judgment was coming but that God had provided a way of salvation to all who would believe and trust in Him. But they were so immersed in their materialistic lives and pleasures that they ignored the WARNING SIGNS and got taken by surprise. Noah disappeared into the Ark before the judgments of the flood fell and took them all away. Likewise the Church will be raptured (disappear) before the judgements of the Tribulation fall upon all the earth.

God gave them the SIGN of METHUSELAH (as well as the visual aid of the Ark). Enoch the prophet warned of the flood and named his son Methuselah meaning: **"when he dies it shall come."** He was the Time-Clock for the Flood. His 'passing away' was the deadline for the Flood.
The Clock started at his birth and ran for his lifetime. As he grew older he was a sign that the Flood was approaching soon, bringing a new dispensation. Methuselah gave the general but not the exact time of the Flood.

The very year Methuselah died the Flood came!
Methuselah was 187 when Lamech was born (Genesis 5:25)
Lamech was 182 when Noah was born (Genesis 5:28)
Noah was 600 when the Flood came (Genesis 7:6)
Now 187 + 182 + 600 = 969 years.
And Methuselah lived 969 years! (Genesis 5:27)
God's grace is seen in that Methuselah lived the longest of all men.

So they had a Sign and a Time-Clock just as we have the Fig-Tree (Israel). Theirs was the life-span of an individual; ours is the life-span of the generation who saw the Fig-Tree spring up.

All these signs give the general time of the end (of the approaching start of the Tribulation), however the exact timing is not given: **"but of that** (exact) **day and hour** (of the start of the 'end of the age'- see Question 3) **no one knows, not even the angels of heaven, but My Father only"** (Matthew 24:36).
God has kept this day (the start of the Day of the Lord) secret so that we always stay ready. In fact Jesus says life will be going on as normal for the world and

they will be taken by surprise as it was in the days of Noah when the Flood came suddenly upon an unsuspecting world. Jesus will come as a thief in the night to take believers away. There will be no special sign to tell the world the Tribulation is about to start except the Rapture itself and then it will be too late. This is in contrast to the Second Coming, for the Bible gives a clear calendar of events by which someone in the Tribulation could know exactly the date of the Lord's Return. Moreover life at the end of the Tribulation, at the time of Armageddon, will be far from normal as the Book of Revelation makes clear. So there is a quite different set of signs for the Tribulation than the Second Coming.

After giving the general signs of the Fig-Tree and all the Trees, Jesus then gave the final sign that would happen just before the Tribulation starts - the RAPTURE OF THE TRUE CHURCH. Luke 21:28 connects these signs with the Rapture: **"Now when these things begin to happen, look up and lift up your heads, because your redemption** (the resurrection of the body in the Rapture) **draws near."** The Church is restraining the final manifestation of evil (2Thessalonians 2:6-8). So the disappearance of the Church will result in the sudden release of evil causing the Tribulation to begin. Revelation confirms that in the Tribulation evil comes to its fullness and is then judged by God. Thus the Rapture is the final sign to the world that the Tribulation is about to start. No one can know the day of the Rapture and the start of the Tribulation.

SIGN (3): The RAPTURE

Matthew 24:37-44: **"But as the days of Noah, so also will the Coming of the Son of Man be. For as in the days before the flood, they were eating and drinking, marrying and giving in marriage, until the day that Noah entered the Ark, and did not know until the Flood came and took them all away, so also will the Coming of the Son of Man be. Then two men will be in the field: one will be taken and the other left. Two women will be grinding at the mill: one will be taken and the other left. Watch therefore, for you do not know what hour your Lord is coming. But know this, that if the master of the house had known what hour**

the thief would come, he would have watched and not allowed his house to be broken into. Therefore you also be ready, for the Son of Man is coming at an hour you do not expect."

The context for this passage is not the Second Coming. After v27, the subject changed to when the Tribulation would start. Those who apply this to the 2nd Coming either see a Post-Tribulation Rapture or the removal of unbelievers in judgment in v40,41. The Coming of the Lord described in Matt 24:36-44 is not His Second Coming in power and glory, but His secret unannounced coming as a thief in the night. The Day of the Lord (Tribulation) starts with Him coming to His Church as her Bridegroom to take her home and it ends with Him coming with His Church as King of Kings. This is the first and therefore foundational Biblical passage on the Rapture. Its context is as part of the answer to the question about the signs for the Tribulation. Therefore, Jesus teaches a Rapture of believers before the Tribulation. Some deny this on the basis that the Rapture is part of the Mystery that was only revealed through the Apostle Paul. But it was Jesus who started revealing the mystery near the end of His ministry (Matthew 13), including the Church (Matthew 16) and the Rapture (John 14:1-3). Paul was called to bring the revelation of the Mystery to completion.

The subject is the start of the Tribulation (v36), also described as the Coming of the Son of Man (v37,39,44). He comes like a thief (v43) and removes the believers from the earth (v40,41). This is the Rapture. No one knows when He will come and release the unsuspecting world into the Tribulation (v36,39, 42,44). That time has many parallels with the days of Noah (v37).

1. Conditions will be similar - the world will be ripe for judgement.

2. Normal life will be going on until the very day it happens (v38,40,41).

3. God provided an escape for believers. The Ark is a picture of Christ. In the Ark, Noah was protected from judgment, and was lifted up ABOVE the Flood waters. Likewise, true believers in Christ will be safe. They will be lifted up above the Flood of Judgements.   The believers in Noah's time were removed to safety before judgment fell.   So the Church will be removed by the Rapture

before the Tribulation starts (v40,41). <u>As Noah was removed before the judgments of the Flood suddenly fell on the world, so the Church will be removed before the judgments of the Tribulation suddenly fall upon the whole earth</u>.

As Noah's family disappeared into the Ark before judgment fell, so the true believers will be raptured (taken to safety) before the Tribulation judgments fall upon all the unbelieving world.   This is because the Tribulation is a time of God's wrath and judgment and God always provides deliverance from judgment for His people. A Kingdom always pulls out its ambassadors before it wages war. They are all taken home and then judged and rewarded for their service in that foreign land. As soon as they are safe, judgment falls. Likewise as soon as God pulls out His ambassadors in the Rapture, judgement (the Tribulation) will fall.

4. The final sign for the world that the Flood was about to fall was the disappearance of the believers.   Likewise the sign for the world that the Tribulation is about to start will be the Rapture (disappearance) of the Church. God shut the door signifying it was then too late for the rest to escape. So also, when the Rapture happens and believers go through an open door into Heaven, the door will shut and there is no escape for the rest of the world who must go through the Tribulation (Luke 21:35,36).

5. The very day Noah entered the Ark judgement fell (v38,39; Genesis 7:13). The unknown day of the Coming of the Lord as a thief (the Rapture) is identified as the very same day the Tribulation begins. See 1Thessalonians 5:1,2.

<u>Luke 17:28-30 is a similar passage:</u> **"As it was also in the days of Lot: they ate, they drank, they bought, they sold, they planted, they built; but <u>on the day</u> that Lot went out of Sodom it rained fire and brimstone from heaven and destroyed them all. Even so will it be in the day when the Son of Man is revealed."** Again we see that the very day Lot escaped judgement fell.   Jesus says it will be the same at the Rapture. As soon as His people are removed there is nothing to stop God moving in judgement.

6. The Flood was a world-wide judgement, so also the Tribulation (v39). This is confirmed in a Luke 21:34-36, which is part of this comparison passage

with the days of Noah: **"Take heed to yourselves, lest ...** <u>that Day</u> (the start
of the Tribulation) **come on you unexpectedly. For it will come as a snare
on** <u>all those who dwell on the face of the whole earth</u> (like the Flood).
**Watch therefore and pray always that you may be counted worthy
to escape** (like Noah) **all these things that shall come to pass**
(in the Tribulation)**, and to stand before the Son of Man** (in the Rapture)**."**

7. They did not know when the Flood would come until it did (v39).
Likewise no one can know when the Rapture is (v42,44). There is no special
warning sign. <u>This passage teaches that the Rapture is imminent</u> - that is -
it could happen at any time. As those in the time of Noah could know the
general time of the Flood from Methuselah ('when he dies it shall come') we
know we are in the general time from the Fig-Tree ('the generation that sees
her put forth her leaves again shall not pass away'). Although these signs tell us
we are in the general time of the end, no one knows the day or hour of the
Rapture and the start of the Tribulation. Only God knows when - the exact time
is hidden from humanity (v36,42,44). This is so we get and stay ready.

<u>Therefore, there will be no special signs preceding the Rapture,</u> as there will be
before the Second Coming. The Flood came during normal conditions on earth
with men eating, drinking, and marrying. All these are normal human activities,
not sinful in themselves. Likewise the Rapture will come at a time when things
are normal on the earth. People will be at their normal work,
not suspecting that something major is about to happen (v40,41).
This is clearly not true for the Second Coming as the Book of Revelation shows.
Thus God has made the Rapture imminent so that we be always ready.

**"Then two men will be in the field: one will be taken and the other left.
Two women will be grinding at the mill: one will be taken, the other left"**
(v40,41). The believers are taken by the thief in the night - Jesus Christ.
In v43, Jesus describes this event for the first time as a thief in the night, who
comes and goes unseen by the unbelieving owner (v43) and whenever this
phrase is used later, it refers to the Rapture. To the world, Jesus will come as

a thief in the night taking the precious things from the earth. A thief comes unannounced, at a time you don't expect, with no warning signs.

Paul in 1Thessalonians 5:1,2 expounds this prophecy of Jesus:
"**The Day of the Lord** (the Tribulation) **so comes** (begins) **as a thief in the night** (the Rapture). **For when they say, "Peace and safety!"**
(there will be no special warning- normal conditions on earth)
then sudden destruction comes upon them, as labour pains upon a pregnant woman (the Tribulation). **And they shall not escape."**
The whole world will suffer. It will be too late to be part of the Rapture.
As God shut the door when Noah entered the Ark, so the door into Heaven will be shut immediately after the Rapture. The thief removes something that must be a restraining force, resulting in a sudden onset of destruction.

WHO IS TAKEN in v40,41? Some say that it is the unbelievers who are taken from the earth (by death) as in v39, and that this passage refers to the Second Coming. However, this event happens at the Judgement of the Sheep and Goats (Matthew 25) when everyone is standing before Christ, not while they are at work. Moreover, the Greek word used for 'took' in v39 is completely different from 'taken' in v40 and 41. Verse 39 describes the unbelievers taken away by the Flood. The word means to be swept away, as in judgement. On the other hand, the word used for 'taken' in v40,41 means 'to take to be with someone' as in Matthew 1:20: **"Joseph, son of David, do not be afraid to TAKE to** (be with) **you Mary your wife, for that which is conceived in her is of the Holy Spirit"**, and Matthew 17:1 **"Now after six days Jesus TOOK** (to be with him) **Peter, James, and John his brother, led them up on a high mountain by themselves."** See also Matthew 18:16; 20:17. So this is talking about Jesus, coming for His Bride and taking us to be with Himself. It is exactly what Jesus talks about in John 14:2,3 which is the next time He describes the Rapture: **"In My Father's house are many mansions; if it were not so, I would have told you. I go to prepare a place for you. And if I go and prepare a place for you, I will come again and receive you to Myself; that where I am, there you may be also."** It is for salvation, not judgement.

'That Day' in Matthew 24:36 is the same as 'that Day' in Luke 21:34, which is then described and defined in Luke 21:35,36 as the first Day of the Tribulation the opening of **the Day of the Lord** when 'all these things' will come to pass, but from which an escape is provided for believers. This confirms that the time under discussion from v36 is the Rapture and start of the Tribulation.

In Matthew 24:36-44, Jesus is telling us to watch (to be ready) so that we will escape the Tribulation, by going up in the Rapture. Noah was ready, but the others carried on, oblivious to the threat of judgement. Noah was removed to safety, they were swept away. You can prepare and be ready like Noah or just carry on like the rest. Those who were ready were those who were saved. Those who were lost were the unprepared. Likewise at the Rapture there is a separation into two groups (v40,41). Some will be ready, some will not. Believers will be removed to safety and soon after, the judgements of the Tribulation will come upon the whole world.

In view of these things Jesus warns us: **"Watch therefore, for you do not know what hour your Lord is coming. But know this, that if the master of the house had known what hour the thief would come, he would have watched... Therefore you also be ready, for the Son of Man is coming at an hour you do not expect"** (Matthew 24:42-44).
Likewise He says: **"Take heed (be alert) WATCH and PRAY for you know not what hour your Lord shall come"** (Mark 13:33). WATCH and discern the signs of the times (know that we live in the last generation). This will keep us spiritually alert and praying, staying ready for the Lord's Return.

Then follows Matthew 24:45-51, a parable teaching that watchful readiness is to be busy labouring not just passively looking at the sky. The judgement on the unbeliever (in v21) who is not ready for the Rapture is executed at the Second Coming. This is the transition to Matthew 25 which starts: **"Then shall the Kingdom of heaven be like..."** Thus the point in time of the judgements of Matthew 25 is the Second Coming (not the Rapture). In the midst of describing these judgements Jesus warns those living before the Rapture to be ready for His Coming so that they may escape these judgements (v13)

Luke states this warning of Jesus very clearly in Luke 21:34-36: **"But take heed to yourselves, lest at any time your hearts be weighed down** (overcharged) **with carousing** (dissipation)**, drunkenness and cares of this life, and so that Day** (the DAY of the Lord -Tribulation) **come on you unexpectedly. For it will come as a snare on all those who dwell on the face of the whole earth** (do not be like those in Noah's time who ignored the preacher and got destroyed in the flood). **"WATCH therefore** (for the SIGNS - let them alert you that Jesus is Coming soon and live accordingly - get ready!) **and PRAY always** (do not be spiritually asleep - prayerless, absorbed in the cares and pleasures of this life) **that you may be counted worthy** (ready) **to escape** (in the Pre-Tribulational Rapture) **all these things that shall come to pass** (in the Tribulation)**, and to stand** (resurrected) **before the Son of man"** (in Heaven- by means of Rapture) This is not just a protection from the troubles but an escape from them by being moved out of the world to stand before the Son of Man. This can only be done by the Rapture before the Tribulation. Jesus taught a Pre-Tribulation Rapture.

In fact at the Rapture we shall all stand before Christ and His Judgement Seat , when we will be judged as Servants for rewards. This provides extra motivation to stay ready for the Lord's imminent coming and occupied in His service:

Mark 13:34-37: **"It is like a man** (Jesus) **going to a far country** (heaven)**, who left his house and gave authority to his servants, and to each his work, and commanded the doorkeeper to watch. Watch therefore, for you do not know when the master of the house is coming--in the evening, at midnight, at the crowing of the rooster, or in the morning- lest, coming suddenly, he find you sleeping. And what I say to you, I say to all: Watch!"** This is His Coming in the Rapture because believers in the Tribulation should know exactly when He will return.

HOW TO BE READY

(1) Receive Jesus as your Lord and Saviour.
The main way we get ready is receiving and trusting Jesus Christ and His death on the Cross as our salvation, and following Him as our Lord.

(2) Prove the genuineness of your faith by a changed life.

Those who carried on same life in Noah's time proved their unbelief by their lifestyle, they were not ready because they did not believe. Some may have professed faith but it was an empty profession because it did not change their life. They carried on oblivious to Noah's warnings.

Are there other indications that Jesus will come in our generation?

(1) PETER gives us a clue. When speaking of the time-period left before the end and the TIMING of the Lord's Return, he gives the key: **"With the Lord ONE DAY is as 1000 years and 1000 years as ONE DAY"** (2Peter 3:8). History is modelled on the CREATION WEEK of 7 DAYS = 7000 years. God counts time in sevens and the Creation Week is a Type of a WEEK of history = 7000 years.   We stand at the end of 6 DAYS = 6000 years and therefore the final SABBATH DAY OF REST (1000 years, the Millennium - see Revelation 20) is about to begin when Jesus, the Lord of the Sabbath will rule (Mark 2:28).

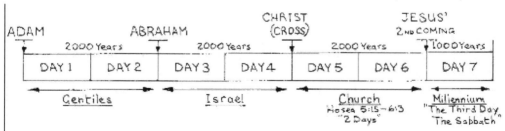

(2) HOSEA'S PROPHECY OF 2000 years (Hosea 5:14-6:3).

Hosea saw the cutting down of Israel and her restoration.

"I (Messiah) **will be like a LION to Ephraim and like a young LION to the house of Judah."** Jesus came as their KING but they reject Him - therefore:

"I even I will tear them (cut them off) **and GO AWAY** (back to Heaven).

I will take them away (from the land) **and none shall rescue.**

I will return to my place (the ascension to the right hand of God the Father)

UNTIL (this implies He will return after a time) **they acknowledge**

their offence (the specific sin of rejecting Him as their King).

Then they will seek My face. In their TRIBULATION they will earnestly

seek Me (saying): "Come, let us return to the Lord, for He has torn,
but He will heal us.   He has stricken but He will bind us up" (these are
the words their leaders will use to call Israel back to accept Jesus as Christ).

Next, He gives a clue as to how long it will be before Christ returns to restore
Israel. "AFTER 2 DAYS (2000 years) He will revive us. On the 3rd DAY (the
1000 year Millennium) He will raise us (Israel) up that we may live in His
sight. Let us know, let us press on to know the Lord. His going forth (out
of Heaven in His 2nd Coming) is established (certain and at a fixed time) as the
morning *sunrise* (He comes as the Sun of Righteousness to start a new DAY of
human history. What is the fixed, appointed time? AFTER 2 DAYS = 2000 years
from His ascension to Heaven in AD 33). He will come to us as the rain, like
the latter and former rain on the earth" (spiritual blessings in the Millennium).

So, Hosea 5:15-6:3 speaks of Christ being rejected, then going to Heaven for
TWO DAYS (2000 years) before returning to a repentant Israel to reign over
them for the THIRD DAY (1000 years, see Revelation 20).

We are presently near the end of 2000 years from His First Coming!
There were 4 DAYS (4000 years) from Adam to the Cross. Here Hosea predicts
there will be 2 DAYS (2000 years) from the Cross to the Second Coming.
This makes 6 DAYS, leaving 1 more DAY of 1000 years, the Sabbath DAY of
rest, the Millennium, the 3rd DAY of Hosea's prophecy.
Therefore we stand near the end of 2000 years from the Cross and we see
Israel restored to the land in preparation to be restored to the Lord!

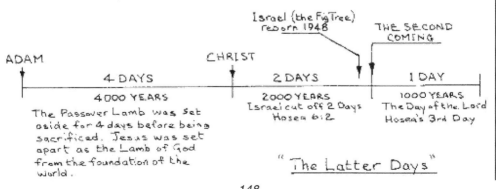

148

Framework Prophecy 3

The Revelation to John

The Book of Revelation is the climax of the whole Bible. It brings God's Word to its completion as its final words confirm (Revelation 22:18,19). Therefore it has a place of special importance in God's Word. Every theme and revelation of the Bible has its roots and origins in Genesis, develops progressively and then comes to its completion in Revelation. The Book of Revelation therefore brings together these themes and shows how they will all come to their fulfillment.

It is of course a Book of Prophecy, and so in it all the various streams of Bible Prophecy are brought together, revealing how all things will come to their climax, and especially how God's Plans and Purposes come to their ultimate fulfillment. **Therefore the Book of Revelation is essential to understanding Prophecy**. This is why Book 3 of this Series is devoted to it.

Its very name 'Revelation' implies it is written to clearly reveal what is to happen in the future. Throughout the Bible are scattered many different prophecies, but without Revelation we would have great difficulty fitting them all together to see in detail what is going to come to pass. It ties together all the prophetic threads and adds the necessary detail to complete what was missing in the previous prophetic revelation of God. It takes the former prophecies and combines them with new revelation based on John's vision of the future, to present a coherant and orderly and chronological portrayal of the end-times. It shows exactly how and when the various prophecies will come to pass and fills in any remaining gaps of knowledge left by the incompleteness of previous revelation.

Therefore, as the ultimate word of prophecy, concluding and summarising the revelation of the Bible, we would expect Revelation to provide a systematic Framework into which all the various prophetic pieces are seen to be fitted. This is exactly what we find. The structure of the Book of Revelation provides confirmation of the overall Framework we have developed in this book. It is also the Book that gives us a detailed chronological Framework for the Tribulation.

Revelation 1:19 gives the outline of the whole Book: **"Write the things**
(1) Which YOU HAVE SEEN (1:1-19 - John's vision of Christ)
(2) the things THAT ARE NOW (1:20-3:22 - the Church-Age)
(3) the THINGS THAT WILL TAKE PLACE AFTER THIS (after the Church-Age-chapters 4-22). As we read on, we see that the things after the Church-Age are: The Church raptured to Heaven as the Tribulation is about to begin (chap 4,5), The Tribulation on earth, a terrible time of evil and Divine judgement (chap 6-18) The Second Coming of Christ to end the Tribulation (ch 19), the Millennial (1000 year) reign of Christ and Final Judgement (ch 20), The Eternal State (ch 21,22).

Chapters 2 and 3 give an overview of the Church Age ('the things that are now'). At the end of chapter 3, there is a clear change signalled by John being taken up to Heaven in 4:1 (a picture of the Rapture of the Church). This indicates we are now in the next stage of the revelation ('the things that will take place after this'). Revelation 4:1 confirms this: **"AFTER THESE THINGS** ('the things that are now' -the Church-Age) **I looked and behold a door standing open in heaven, and the first voice which I heard was like a trumpet speaking with me saying, 'Come up here and I will show you THINGS WHICH MUST TAKE PLACE AFTER THIS."** This proves the present Church Age ends after chapter 3 and that 'the things that will take place after this' (including the Tribulation) start in chapter 4. Thus the Church-Age ends before the Tribulation begins. The Tribulation is seen as a future dispensation that comes AFTER the Church-Age. This is confirmed by the resurrected Church (represented by the 24 elders) being in Heaven in chapters 4-5. Chapters 4-22 happen after the Church-Age.

The prophetic Framework as revealed by the structure of the Book of Revelation
1. **THE RISEN CHRIST - His First Coming** (chapter 1).
2. **THE CHURCH AGE** (chapters 2 and 3).
3. **THE CHURCH RAPTURED AND IN HEAVEN** (chapters 4,5)
4. **THE TRIBULATION** (chapters 6-18).
5. **THE SECOND COMING OF CHRIST** (chapter 19).
6. **THE MILLENNIUM** (chapter 20).
7. **THE ETERNAL STATE** (chapters 21 and 22).

Key 12: Futurism.

The study of 'the last things' is called eschatology (*'eschatos'* = last). Unfortunately the church worls has differed greatly in how to interpret these scriptures. We conclude our study of the key principles of interpreting prophecy, by summarising the 4 main schools of interpretation that have arisen in Church history. They differ in how and when Revelation 4-22 and Matthew 24:7-31 will be fulfilled. Are these predictions past, present or future to us who live almost 2000 years after they were made? Most books on prophecy will be written from the standpoint of one of these schools.

1. The PRETERIST school believes that these prophecies were mostly fulfilled in the first few centuries after Christ. They were written to help the first century Christians to prepare them for what was shortly going to happen. However it seems clear that these prophecies have not come to pass yet in any literal sense, so this school depends on very loose, poetic interpretations. Moreover it means that the Book of Revelation has very little relevance for us today.

2. The HISTORICIST school seeks to make Revelation more relevant by saying the predictions cover the whole Church Age. It gives us a symbolic coded prophecy of the Church Age, and so in Revelation we can see the events of the last 2000 years unfold, we can trace the course of Church history. However the suggested fulfilments are artificial and unconvincing, again requiring a non-literal interpretation of prophecy.

3. The IDEALIST view removes all time references and discourages us seeing specific fulfilments. Instead Revelation portrays the eternal struggle betwen good and evil, and we can apply its truths at any time. In other words it treats prophecy as myth- describing fictional events that carry a moral or spiritual meaning. This amounts to a denial of the truth of God's Word and a denial of such events as the Second Coming and the Final Judgement.

4. The FUTURIST view (which is expounded in this Book) is based on taking prophecy literally (using the same rules of interpretation as other area of doctrine). That is we take it in its plain meaning, which means literally unless there is obvious symbolism or figures of speech being used. If the literal meaning makes sense then read it that way.   Applying this principle it is clear that Revelation 4-22 has not yet been fulfilled, it still awaits a future fulfilment. Most of end-time prophecy describes the climax of the battle between good and evil over this world.   In this way we don't have to make forced interpretations of prophecies to show how they have already been fulfilled.

One criticism of FUTURISM is that the prophecies do not apply to us today, and so studying prophecy has little value for us.   However this is shortsighted. The same argument could be used to say it is pointless to study Bible history, since prophecy is just His-story that has not happened yet! As we come to know what God has done and what He will do, we discover His character, power and purposes and how we fit into the scheme of things and how we are to focus our lives. Understanding what lies ahead stabilises us in difficult times when evil just seems to be increasing.   We know what is happening and we know God wins! He is working His purposes out.   Knowing what will happen strengthens and guides us for our life now. The key things we need in life are faith, HOPE and love and hope is only developed through the study of Bible Prophecy. Our hope in the soon Coming of Christ keeps us watchful, alert and occupied in His work.

More specifically, by showing us the end of this age in great detail the Bible helps us to interpret what is happening around us, for this world is necessarily moving closer and closer to the conditions described in Revelation.
This helps us understand the forces at work around us, so that we can unmask the disguises of evil and discern and give ourselves to what God is doing.
By comparing our generation to Revelation we can see we live close to the end. So end-time prophecy very much applies to our life today.

We will also see prophecies that apply to this present age. Moreover by applying TYPOLOGY to some literal prophecies (without denying their primary literal fulfilment), we will gain prophetic insights into our present time.   In Book 2 we will do this with the 7 Churches in Revelation 2 and 3.   In Book 3 we will do this for the 7 TIMES (of the Gentiles) in Daniel 4. But this is quite different from taking a HISTORICIST approach to interpreting prophecy.

Appendix 1 : Daniel's 70 Weeks

A critique of Sir Robert Anderson's interpretation in 'The Coming Prince'
and Harold Hoehner's revision in 'Chronological Aspects of the Life of Christ.'

Daniel's Seventy Weeks is a vital foundational Bible prophecy that requires careful study to understand properly, as Jesus said when commenting upon it, "let those who read it understand" (Matthew 24:15). This chronological prophecy predicts the time of the Coming of Christ and should be fulfilled exactly (to the day). The correct interpretation sheds much light on the rest of Bible Prophecy, so it is important that we seek to find it.

In this book, I have presented what I am sure is the right interpretation which was first discerned by Sir Edward Denney, which leads to an exact fulfillment to the day, as I shall show.   But unfortunately sometimes the greatest barrier to the truth is something close to the truth which satisfies us, so that we fail to dig deeper. In the case of Daniel's Seventy Weeks those who look for a literal and exact fulfillment think they have already found it in the well-known work of Sir Robert Anderson's *The Coming Prince*, revised and updated by Harold Hoehner who changed Anderson's starting and finishing years by a year.   This interpretation has encouraged many who believe in the literal fulfillment of prophecy and so it is with reluctance that in the interests of truth I have to reveal that it is undeniably incorrect in a number of ways.

The Anderson interpretation claims to provide an accurate fulfillment to the very day. As a result people think it can't possibly be wrong. Moreover they are unable to check the validity of the calculation due to the large number (173,880) of days involved (however with calendar software available on the internet it is now fairly straightforward to do this) Unfortunately, when the calculation is checked it does not work as claimed. It is better that people realise this, rather than be misled by an incorrect and inferior interpretation which only has an apparent accuracy. Their heart will then be open to hear and receive the true literal fulfillment of the 70 Weeks. If they remain attached to Anderson's interpretation they will fail to find the full understanding of Daniel's 70 Weeks.

So, the following critique is written for those who find it hard to receive the interpretation in this book, because of their commitment to Anderson's more well-known interpretation.   My reason in pulling it down is only to put something much better in its place, for if we do not have an accurate understanding of the Seventy Weeks our grasp of Bible Prophecy and Chronology will be greatly hindered.

The 70 Weeks (Daniel 9:24-27).

v24: **"70 weeks** (490 years) **are determined for your people** (Israel) **and for your holy city** (Jerusalem),
(1) To finish the transgression, (2) to make an end of sins,
(3) To make reconciliation (atonement) **for iniquity** (fulfilled at the Cross in AD33),
(4) To bring in (the kingdom of) **everlasting righteousness,**
(5) To seal up (fulfil) **vision and prophecy,**
(6) and to anoint the Most Holy (Temple) (Yet to be fulfilled)."

v25: **"Know therefore and understand, that from the going forth of the** (Divine) **command** ('dabar') **to restore and build Jerusalem until Messiah the Prince,** *there shall be* 7 weeks (49 years) **and 62 weeks** (434 years); (making a total of 483 years). **The street shall be built again, and the wall, even in troublesome times** (fulfilled in the time of Ezra-Nehemiah)."

v26: **"And after the 62 weeks** (after 483 years) **the Messiah shall be cut off** (by capital punishment), **but not for Himself** (or: 'but He shall have nothing, His kingdom will be unrealised'); **and the people** (Romans) **of the prince who is to come** (antichrist) **shall destroy the city** (Jerusalem) **and the sanctuary** (the Temple) **the end of it** *shall be* **with a flood, and till the end of the war desolations are determined** (fulfilled AD 66-73)."

v27 The future Tribulation: **"Then he** (the antichrist, the prince who is to come) **shall confirm a covenant with many for one week** (7 years); **but in the middle of the week** (after 3.5 yrs) **he shall bring an end to sacrifice and offering. And on the wing of abominations shall be one who makes desolate** (he will set up the Abomination of Desolation in the Temple) **even until the consummation which is determined, is poured out on the desolate** (he will be destroyed at the end of the 7 years)."

Firstly I should point out that as far as the substance of Anderson's dispensational interpretation is concerned, I am in agreement. What is under discussion here is the chronology- the detailed timing of how it was and will be fulfilled. This is a chronological prophecy and so to interpret it properly we must understand its time measurements accurately. Key questions are: (1) When do the 490 years start and end?, and (2) What kind of year is being used?

1. I will first summarise Anderson's interpretation.
2. Then I will reveal its errors.
3. Then I will summarise Hoehner's improved version.
4. Then I will show how this also is fatally flawed.
5. Finally I will show that although these both fail to give an exact fulfillment to the day, the true interpretation succeeds.

1. Anderson claims to have found the exact fulfillment (to the very day) **of Daniel's 70 Weeks.** Anderson noticed that the 70th Week has yet to be fulfilled (Daniel 9:27), so he divided the first 69 weeks (483 years) from the 70th week (7 years), even though Daniel 9:24 considers them as a continuous unbroken series of 490 years. To make his calculation work he used a year of 360 days which he calls a 'prophetic year.'
Now 483 'prophetic' years of 360 days makes 173,880 days.

Anderson took as his starting point Artaxerxes' 20th year of reign, when Nehemiah requested and received permission from the King to continue the rebuilding of the walls of Jerusalem.   His date for 20th Artaxerxes was 445 BC. Nehemiah 2:1 says it was in the month Nisan that Nehemiah received his commission from Artaxerxes. Anderson assumed this meant Nisan 1, and then calculated it as **March 14th, BC 445** (Julian) based on it being a New Moon. He counted 173,880 days from this date of March 14th. He did this by converting this to 476 (Gregorian) years and 24 days (a Gregorian year is 365.242 days), which the reader can easily verify ends on April 6th AD 32 (Julian), which he claimed was Nisan 10th AD 32, the date of the Triumphal Entry (4 days before the Cross)

Since this was Jesus' official Presentation of Himself to Israel as the Messiah this seems to be an impressive end-point of the 483 years. At this point God stopped the prophetic clock for Israel, and will only start it again when the Tribulation begins and the last (70th) Week of 7 years will run to complete the 490 years of Daniel's prophecy.

I remember being impressed by the apparent accuracy of fulfillment (to the day) provided by this interpretation. For this reason many who believe in the literal fulfillment of Bible Prophecy accept Anderson's calculation. However as we shall see, when one looks at the calculation in more detail, one finds it is in error on practically every level.

Anderson explains his calculation: *"The Julian date of 1st Nisan 445 was the 14th March. 69 weeks of years (i.e. 173,880 days) reckoned from the 14th March B.C. 445, ended on the 6th April A.D. 32.   Now 483 years (69 x 7) of 360 days contain 173,880 days. And a period of 173,880 days, beginning March 14th, B.C. 445, ended upon that Sunday in the week of the crucifixion . . or Palm Sunday. The Julian date of that 10th Nisan was Sunday the 6th April, A.D32. What then was the length of the period intervening between the issuing of the decree to rebuild Jerusalem and the public advent of "Messiah the Prince" — between the 14th March, B.C.445, and the 6th April, AD32? THE INTERVAL CONTAINED EXACTLY and to the VERY DAY 173,880 DAYS, or 7 TIMES 69 PROPHETIC YEARS of 360 DAYS, the first 69 weeks of Gabriel's prophecy."*

2. Sir Robert Anderson's theory doesn't work!

*Wrong Intervening Period. There is a serious calculation error hidden in his mixing of 2 calendars, which by itself invalidates his calculation. There is a confusion between Julian and Gregorian calendars. The Julian calendar is longer than a true solar year (about 3 days in 4 centuries).   This error amounted to 11 days in AD. 1752 when our English calendar was corrected by declaring the 3rd September to be the 14th September, and by introducing the Gregorian reform, so that the Gregorian calendar we now use stays in line with the sun.

The problem is that Anderson uses *Gregorian* years when calculating the number of days between two *Julian* dates. If we use Julian dates, we must also use Julian years, and if we use Gregorian dates, we must use Gregorian years. We cannot mix the two calendars in the way that he proposes. Anderson was thus 3 days off in his calculation, for there are really 173,883 days inclusive between Friday, March 14, 445 BC and Sunday, April 6, 32AD (Julian). Instead of adding 116 days for leap years, Anderson should have added 119, for that is precisely how many leap years there are in 476 years in the Julian calendar. If he had wanted to use Gregorian years, he should have started and ended with the Gregorian dates of Saturday, March 9, 445 BC, and Sunday, April 4, 32 AD (March 9, 445BC Gregorian = March 14, 445BC Julian; April 4, 32AD Gregorian = April 6,

32AD Julian). But when we add 116 days for leap years to the number of days between these   2 dates, we still end up with 173,883 days. Only by mixing the two calendars does it falsely appear that there are 173,880 days.

*<u>**Wrong Day to Start From.**</u> Jewish months back then, began when the new moon could just be seen with the naked eye soon after sunset. At sunset on the evening of March 13th the moon would have been only 11 hours old, too young to be seen. **Thus the new month could not have begun until the   evening of March 14th, making March 15th the first day   of the new month, not March 14**[th] as Anderson has it.

*<u>**Wrong Month to Start From.**</u> March 14th Julian (March 9th Gregorian) is too early in the year to be considered Nisan 1st. We have 2 resources that tell us something about the calendar back in the 5th century BC: Jewish scribal papyri from Elephantine, Egypt and cuneiform tablets from Mesopotamia . Both indicate that March 14 is too early in the year to be considered Nisan, the first month of the Jewish year (see Appendix). **Thus in 445 BC, Nisan would have begun after the new moon of April, not after the new moon of March, making April 13 the true Nisan 1, not March 14.** It is questionable if the barley could have been ripe enough for the wave sheaf offering on Nisan 16 if Nisan 1 was as early as March 14. That date is just too early in the year.

*<u>**Wrong Year to Start From**</u>. The main purpose of this article is that Anderson's calculation is demonstrably wrong from a technical point of view, but it is appropriate to also mention that his candidate for the starting year of Daniel's 70 Weeks (Nisan 445 BC), the 20th year of Artaxerxes (Nehemiah 2), does not agree well with the description of Daniel 9:25: **"from the going forth of the command** (decree of divine origin - 'dabar') **to restore and build Jerusalem."**

The prophecy should really be tied to Artaxerxes' 7th year -Nisan 458 BC (Ezra 7) not his 20th year. **The simple fact is that there is no decree recorded from the 20th year of Artaxerxes in the book of Nehemiah!** The earlier decrees of Cyrus (Ezra 1:2-4) and Darius (Ezra 6:1-12) focused on the building of the Temple, but it is only in Artaxerxes' decree in his 7th year, as recorded in Ezra 7, that there is a restoration   of the judiciary (self-government).   At the start of his reign, Artaxerxes ordered that Jerusalem could not be rebuilt with walls until he gave the command (Ezra 4:21, see also v11-16). This command was then given in Ezra 7 in his 7th year (458 BC), where the king makes a decree which clearly has divine origin coming directly from God's throne (v27) as the word 'dabar' requires. This decree imparted full authority to Israel for self-government, so that it could function as a city (under the Persian Empire). This command also gave them authority to rebuild the walls of Jerusalem as Ezra 9:9 explicitly tells us.

This is also a logical consequence from the context of the Ezra 7 decree. For it was the reversal of the Ezra 4:21 command made by Artaxerxes in probably his first year, which forbid them rebuilding the city and its wall. Ezra went ahead and developed the spiritual and civil aspects of Israel's government. However fears due to longstanding implacable local opposition to the rebuilding of Jerusalem (see Ezra 4) meant that this rebuilding did not take effect for another 13 years when only the arrival of Nehemiah made it possible, who had both great courage and favour with the Persian King. Through the strong leadership of Nehemiah, Israel was able to overcome their fears and enemies, and implement their authority to rebuild the city.

Nehemiah was galvanized into action in Nehemiah 1 when he received the report that the King's earlier decree (458 BC) had not resulted in the rebuilding of Jerusalem. So he sought and received permission to accomplish this neglected task. **The important issue is that Nehemiah was simply** released by the King to implement an earlier decree. **There is no new decree in the book of Nehemiah!** This is easily checked by reading Nehemiah.

The dominant decree in Ezra-Nehemiah around which all the action is based is the one in Artaxerxes' 7th year (Ezra 7). That's why it is emphasised so strongly and dated so exactly,as if God was underlining it (as anyone can verify by reading it). **Thus the only possible start date for the 70 Weeks is 458BC.** This agrees with the prophecy itself (Daniel 9:24,25) which says there would be a decree to rebuild Jerusalem and that it would be rebuilt as a fortified city within the first 7 Weeks (49 years) in troublous times (against much opposition). Now while Cyrus' decree (537 BC) to rebuild the Temple resulted in the resettlement of Jerusalem this prophecy was not fulfilled in the years (537-488 BC). It was however clearly fulfilled in the days of Ezra-Nehemiah (458 - 409 BC).

*Wrong Day to End With. There are major problems with Anderson's ending date of April 6, 32 AD. His theory called for it to be Nisan 10. He explains it this way: *"For example, in A.D. 32, the date of the true new moon, by which the Passover was regulated, was the night (10h 57m) of the 29th March. The ostensible date of the 1st Nisan, therefore, according to the phases, was the 31st March. It may have been delayed, however, till the 1st April; and in that case the 15th Nisan should apparently have fallen on Tuesday the 15th April."* Thus far his explanation proves that he has chosen the wrong date for the 10th of Nisan. If Nisan 15 fell on April 15, then Nisan 10 fell on April 10, not April 6.

He continues: *"But the calendar may have been further disturbed by intercalation. According to the scheme of the eight years' cycle, the embolismal month was inserted in the third, sixth, and eighth years, and an examination of the calendars from AD.22 to AD. 45 will show that AD. 32 was the third year of such a cycle. As, therefore, the difference between the solar year and the lunar is 11 days, it would amount in three years to 33 3/4 days, and the intercalation of a thirteenth month (Ve-adar) of thirty days would leave an epact still remaining of 3 3/4 days; and the "ecclesiastical moon" being that much before the real moon, the feast day would have fallen on the Friday (11th April), exactly as the narrative of the Gospels requires."*

If that didn't make sense to you, it's because it doesn't make sense. **It is just plain wrong!** The Jews would add in a 13th month every 2 or 3 years.   Since this 13th month was the length of a lunar month, as Anderson admits above, there was no "epact remaining." Thus Nisan 1 would still have begun with observing the new crescent on the evening of March 31st, making April 1st Nisan 1, and April 10th (not April 6th) Nisan 10. **So Nisan 10 occurred at** the earliest on April 10, not April 6 as Anderson supposed.

*Wrong Year to End With.   No one except those who ascribe to Anderson's theory suggests 32 AD as a possible date for the death of Christ. The simple fact is that Nisan 14 (the Cross) in that year would have been on a Monday or Tuesday! **It is simply impossible to reconcile this fact with the Gospel accounts of the death of Christ.   This consideration alone invalidates Anderson's interpretation!**

*Wrong kind of year. Anderson's theory relies on using a 360-day year, which he calls a "prophetic year." Now this can't be right, because this is a prophecy specifically about Israel and would use the kind of year used by Israel, which was a luni-solar year which always stay aligned with the seasons for agricultural and ceremonial reasons (the feasts were connected to their seasons), so that the Passover (14th Nisan) was always kept in the Spring (after the Vernal Equinox on March 20/21st) according to the Biblical requirement (this fact will prove important shortly). Therefore the Jewish year averaged 365.242 days, not 360 days. Anyone reading this prophecy including Daniel would have understood that this kind of year was intended, rather than a 360 day year which Israel never used.

The 360 day year is actually a Babylonian 'Time', and it slips over 5 days a year against the solar seasons, and neither is it in phase with the moon. It is certainly not the year used by Israel. It is misleading to argue that this is the year generally used in the Bible. In fact it is used at most on two specific occasions: the 150 days of Noah's Flood, and the two halves (1260 days each) of the Tribulation. These situations are both special in that they are times of world-wide judgment, and it seems this is when God uses the 360 day year.

That the luni-solar year used by Israel is the year used in the prophecy is confirmed by the fact that the 490 years are described as 70 Weeks (Sevens) of years. This is a clear reference to how God told Israel to count their years in Leviticus 25. They were to mark every 7th year as a Sabbath year when the land was to be rested. Every 7 Sevens of these years was a Jubilee-cycle (49 years), and the 490 years were thought of as 70 Sevens, or 10 Jubilee Cycles of 49 years each on Israel's calendar. Thus the language used alludes to the Jewish Sabbatical and Jubilee cycles that Israel kept according to the Law. We know that the years Israel used and counted in this manner were luni-solar according to God's Law, with each month starting with a new moon and each year starting so that Passover in the first month was in the Spring. These years had to be kept in phase with the solar year, both for agricultural reasons and so that the Feasts (which were connected to the harvests) took place in the right season.

But the 360 day years used by Anderson and Hoehner to make their calculations work neither stay aligned with the seasons, nor the sabbatical cycles. The Passover falls back by 5 days a year and by an entire month every six years. In only 35 years, the Passover would occur in the Fall. Every 70 years, the Passover would have circled all the way through the seasons back to where it started. Thus, there is no possible way to make their calculations align with the years and cycles used by Israel, even though the language used strongly indicates that the prophecy is expressed in terms of these years and cycles. Thus the 360 day calculation is just a hypothetical calculation that bears no resemblence to the years or cycles being used by Israel, and therefore is against the plain meaning of the prophecy. Therefore good Bible interpretation requires us to reject them.

Once we see the 360 day calculation does not work anyway, then all grounds for considering the 360 day year disappear. The only possible way to do justice to the language of the prophecy with the 490 years counted in a way consistent with the Jewish sabbatical system is to use real Jewish luni-solar years that stay aligned with the seasons. Such years must on average be 365.2425 days in length, not 360 days.

Moreover the immediate context of Daniel 9 confirms this. Israel was told that if they did not let the land rest in that 7th year, the land would become desolate and they would be taken captive for a time that would allow the land to have its full quota of rest years that they had not kept (Leviticus 26:34,35). Jeremiah 29:10 later specified that the Jews would be captives in Babylon for 70 years, and this 70 years of desolation is explicitly said to correspond to the number of sabbatical years that had not been kept (2Chron36:21) Thus, Daniel's reference to 70 years of desolation in Daniel 9:2, speaks of a time-period of 490 years during which the land had no sabbaths. So Daniel 9 begins with a reference to a past 490 years or 70 Sevens which had happened, and then ends with a reference to a future period of 490 years or 70 Sevens in the prophecy of the 70 Weeks (Daniel 9:24-27). If the first set of 70x7 years were Jewish luni-solar years then surely the other set of 70x7 years are also to be understood as luni-solar. Thus the context as well as the natural meaning of the language surely tells us that the years in this prophecy are Jewish luni-solar years not Babylonian Times. This is the plain meaning of the prophecy.

3. Dr. Harold Hoehner's Alternative to Anderson's Dates. We've seen that Anderson's calculation is in error on practically every level. Some of these problems are known to dispensational scholars. Dr. H. Hoehner in his book, *Chronological Aspects of the Life of Christ*, presents a different version of Anderson's calculation that gives alternative dates.

This alternative solved some of the difficulties of Anderson's work and it now become widely accepted in dispensational circles. Hoehner's work is based on the same principles as Anderson's, but starts and finishes the 70 Weeks one year later. However we shall see that his calculation does not work either.

The most obvious pointer that Anderson was in error was his year for the crucifixion. Hoehner realised that an AD 32 crucifixion was impossible, for Christ would then have had to die on a Sunday or Monday. Anderson himself realised this dilemma and had to use mental gymnastics to try and get a Friday crucifixion (his attempts to do this are clearly invalid). Hoehner establishes from the criteria that the Crucifixion was on a Friday Nisan 14th that the only possibilities are AD 30 and AD 33. Therefore Hoehner realised the only way to save Anderson's calculation was to bring it forward a year.

Thus instead of having it run from 445 BC - 32 AD, Hoehner's 69 Weeks run from 444 BC - 33AD. His 69 Weeks began on Nisan 1 in 444 BC, which fell on March 5 (Julian). The 69 Weeks then ended on Nisan 10, 33 AD, which fell on March 30 that year. So Christ died on Friday April 3rd (Julian) in 33 AD. Insofar as Hoehner now has the correct date for the Cross, he has improved upon Anderson. However in every other respect his calculation has all the same problems as Anderson's and cannot be correct.

Summary: Hoehner's Four Changes

1. He identified 444 BC as the 20th year of Artaxerxes, however in this respect Anderson was probably right and Hoehner wrong. Both Jewish and Persian practice at that time was to number their years and the years of their kings from Nisan. This gives 445 AD for the 20th year of Artaxerxes which is the generally accepted year (as Anderson used). In order to get 444 BC instead (so that the first 69 Weeks ended in 33AD) he has to argue that the regnal years of Artaxerxes were measured from Tishri on an accession-year system.

2. 33 AD is a much better choice for the year of the crucifixion since it is possible to have Christ die on Friday that year.

3. His starting date, March 5, 444 BC, was the first day of a Jewish month, since the new moon could have first been seen the previous evening. In this respect this is better than Anderson's first day.

4.   His end-date for the first 69 Weeks, March 30, 33 AD, was indeed the tenth day of a Jewish month, since the new crescent moon could have first been seen the evening of March 20. In this respect this is better than Anderson's last day of the 69 Weeks which as we have seen could not have been the 10th of Nisan despite Anderson's claims.

4. We now discuss where Hoehner's calculations fall short.

*Wrong Year to Start From.   As with Anderson, he starts from 20th Artaxerxes (rather than the 7th of Artaxerxes), but he dates it to 444 rather than 445 BC (Anderson). I have previously explained why this change from Anderson is probably in error.
*Wrong kind of year. Like Anderson Hoehner uses the 360 day year which have previously shown to be in error.

*Wrong Intervening Period. Hoehner is guilty of the same basic calculating error as Anderson through mixing together Julian and Gregorian years in his calculation.
Like Anderson, Hoehner converted the 69 Weeks (483 years) of 360 days to days. Multiplying 483 years by 360 days per year gives **173,880 days**, which is about 476 of our (Gregorian) years. He then tries to show that March 5, 444 BC and March 30, 33 AD are 173,880 days apart, which would be exactly 69 Weeks of 360 day years. If this was correct it might be impressive. But it is wrong! **Instead of there being 173,880 days between the dates in question, there are really 173,885 days! Hoehner was off by 5 days in his calculation**! This is an issue of fact not interpretation or opinion.

Any reader can verify this by using a calendar program that computes Julian Day (JD) numbers. (The Julian Day number tells us how many days have transpired since January 1, 4713 BC).   This gives an accurate method of calculating the exact number of days between two dates 476 years apart. One just converts the dates to Julian Days, and then subtracts one from the other to find the precise number of days between the two.   So, March 5, 444 BC (Julian) is JD 1559316, and March 30, 33AD (Julian) is JD 1733200. Thus, by subtraction, reckoning inclusively, there are 173,885 days, NOT 173,880 days. Thus the main strength of this interpretation - its apparent accuracy to the very day - is an illusion.   In the next section we will show it is not only innaccurate but impossible.

How was this error made? In order to determine how many days there were between his start date of March 5, 444 BC (Julian), and his end-date of March 30, 33 AD (Julian), he said this is 476 (solar) years plus 25 days. So he multiplied 476 by 365.24219879, the number of days in a solar year to get 173,855 days and then added 25 days to get the 173,880 days. This would slip under the radar of anyone unfamiliar with calendars. The problem is that he is using Julian dates, but true solar years to measure the gap between them. (A Julian year is only approximately solar, but the difference only builds up over centuries). If he used Julian dates he should have used 365.25, the number of days in a Julian year. Then he would have got the correct answer of 173,885 days between the 2 dates (reckoning inclusively). Or he could have used the Gregorian year with Gregorian dates, but by using the solar 365.24219879 instead of the Julian 365.25 with Julian dates, he introduced confusion resulting in an error of 5 days in his calculation.

It is much safer and less confusing to do these calculations with Julian Day (JD) numbers.

*Wrong Month to Start From. The wrong number of days between March 5, 444 BC, and March 30, 33 AD, is not quite fatal to Hoehner's position, since he correctly states that Artaxerxes could have sent Nehemiah off to Jerusalem later than Nisan 1. If the correct starting date is Nisan 6 instead of Nisan 1, then the number of days between the dates could be 173,880 after all. But the difficulty we will consider in this section disqualifies Hoehner's view from further consideration.

He postulates a Nisan 1 date occurring on March 5, 444 BC. **This corresponds to a Gregorian date of February 28th.** The Gregorian calendar, stays aligned the seasons perpetually. **The Jewish calendar never starts Nisan 1 on February 28** as this is much too early in the year! The Passover would then be on March 13 (Gregorian). However, there is absolutely no way that Jews in 444 BC celebrated the Passover 8 days before the Spring Equinox. This is way too early. It contradicts the Jewish practice as required by the Law of Moses that the Passover (14th Nisan) must be after the Spring Equinox (21st March). **This means that 1st Nisan (Abib) could not possibly be before 8th March (Gregorian).** Moreover if Nisan 1 was on February 28th, then the barley could not possibly be ready for the Firstfruits Offering on Nisan 16th. Thus it is impossible that this could be the starting month for the 70 Weeks, and therefore the whole calculation fails to work, in that it is not just out by a few days, but also by a whole month.

Start a Month Later? We have shown that it is impossible that the New Moon of March 5th (Julian) 444 BC could be Nisan 1 marking the start of the New Year. Therefore Nisan 1 could come no earlier than the next New Moon in 444 BC which was April 3 (Julian). This agrees with today's rabbinical calendar projected back to the 5th century BC.

But this is a whole month later than the date postulated by Hoehner. This means the 69 Weeks finish a month later in 33 AD. That would make Nisan 14 (Passover) fall on Saturday, May 2, or perhaps a day later (Sunday). But if Nisan 14 fell on a Saturday or Sunday in 33 AD, how could Christ have died on a Friday if He died in that year? So when we try to start the 483 years a month later in 444 BC (whatever day in Nisan we start with) we end up with the impossiblilty that Christ died on a Saturday or a Sunday, in 33 AD. So whichever way you try to do it, the Anderson style of calculation does not work. **So, neither Anderson's nor Hoehner's reckoning of the 70 Weeks is correct, and so this interpretation is proven false.**

5. Is there an interpretation of 70 Weeks that works?

The 70th Week is clearly still in the future (Daniel 9:27) and so seems to be divided off from the other 69 Weeks. However the prophecy implies that all 70 Weeks are all together as one unit (v24) with the Messiah bringing Salvation and the Kingdom at the end of the 70th Week (His time starting after 69 Weeks). The failed attempts to make the first 69 Weeks stand alone in measuring the time up to the Cross, confirm that all 70 Weeks should be kept together as one unit. What we have here is a classic prophetic paradox. On one hand, the 70th Week should run straight after the 69th. On the other hand, it is yet future! How can both be true? Rather than choosing one over the other as most interpretations do, let us proceed on the basis that both are true, even if this initially seems impossible!

As we have shown, the starting date for the 70 Weeks is clearly marked in Ezra 7 as Nisan 1, in the 7th year of Artaxerxes. This was without doubt **April 3rd, 458 BC** (Gregorian). Measuring forward 69 Weeks (483 Jewish luni-solar years) takes us to the last day of the 69th Week: April 4th 26AD. This means the 70th Week, the Time of Messiah, began on **April 5th AD 26** with the ministry of John the Baptist. The seven messianic years are in two halves (3.5 years of John the Baptist followed by 3.5 years of the ministry of Jesus Christ). The 70th Week of Messiah is 7 true solar years which close on **April 3rd, AD 33, the very day of His resurrection!** It is also of note that: **490 true solar years from April 3rd, 458BC end on April 1st 33AD, the very day of the Cross!**

This means that the 490 years come to a fitting climax at the death and resurrection of Christ. The 490 years of Daniel 9:24 speak of a Great Jubilee Cycle (10 Jubilees) and so it is a great confirmation that the greatest Jubilee of all (even the fulfilment of all Jubilees - the Cross and Resurrection) took place at the end of a Great Jubilee Cycle. Whereas if the Cross was only after 483 years this would not be true. Only the death and resurrection of Christ form a fitting climax to the 70 Weeks and the calculation works to the very day! In fact the first three of the six supreme messianic accomplishments that v24 tells us should be acheived by the end of the 70th Week were fulfilled at the Cross. Thus we see that by letting all 70 Weeks run their course we get an impressive prophecy of what the Messiah would accomplish in His First Coming, at the climax of the 490 years, and it accurately predicts this to the very day! However, we must also admit there is much in the prophecy that has not been fulfilled in the 490 years from 458BC-33AD, and that the events of the 70th Week are still in the future (v27) How can the prophecy of v24 be fulfilled when the 490 years have passed and the Kingdom not yet established?

It was Sir Edward Denney who discerned the brilliant solution. According to v24, Jesus Christ was ready to fulfil the whole prophecy in 490 years which involved purchasing our salvation and establishing His Kingdom of righteousness on earth (the suffering and the glory). However Israel's rejection of Him as their Messiah-King meant that although He could fulfil the Salvation aspects in His First Coming by His death and resurrection (and did so on time), He was unable to establish His Kingdom at that time. This is indicated in Daniel 9:26: **"He shall be cut off but have nothing"**, that is, His Kingdom shall be unrealised. Thus He fulfilled the first 3 (Salvation) aspects of v24, but He will only fulfil the second 3 (Kingdom) aspects at His 2nd Coming at the end of the future 70th Week described in v27. How can the 70th Week be past and future, fulfilled and unfulfilled? How can we explain this paradox?

The solution is simple: the 70th Week has come and it will come again. It has run, and it will run again at the end. When Israel rejected the King and Kingdom after 7 years of grace, God chronologically cancelled those 7 years (the 70th Week) in order to rerun them at the end of the age as the 7 year Tribulation. He had given Israel 490 years on her clock to fulfil His purposes, but when she rejected Him at the end of the 70 Weeks, God stopped her clock and rewound it 7 years. Meanwhile He brought in a new Body, the Church, for the Church-Age. When the Church Age is ended by the Rapture, Israel's final 7 yrs (the 70th Week) will rerun as the Tribulation. Thus the Messianic Kingdom was postponed 2000 years (40 Jubilees) because of Israel's rejection (just as their entry into the Promised land was postponed 40 years because of unbelief).

These two sets of 7 years concerning Israel are prefigured in Typology by the two periods of 7 years Jacob had to work for a wife and by Joseph's 7 years of plenty and famine:

*The 7 years of prosperity came first, but Israel did not come to Joseph (Jesus) in that time. The dreams show the 7 lean years that came later as eating up the 7 fat years, a perfect description of the what happened to the 70th Week of Grace being replaced (eaten) by the 7 year Tribulation. It is only in the 7 lean years that Israel comes to Joseph (Jesus) and He is revealed to them, and they find salvation through Him.

*Jacob worked 7 years for His wife (Rachel), but at the close of the 7 years he did not obtain her, but another (Leah) came to Him instead. So He had to fulfil another 7 years for Rachel. When the original 7 years ran without fulfilling his purpose, he did not give up on Rachel, but instead reran the 7 years for her. He gave her another Week (of years) of work in the place of the original Week. The first 7 years were not wasted, but as far as Rachel (Israel) was concerned the first 7 years failed to acheive their purpose and so the 7 years for Rachel were run again. The original 7 years were cancelled (as if they had not run) as far as the reckoning for Rachel was concerned. His love for Rachel meant he was willing to run these 7 years again.

This action of God involved both judgement and mercy:
The judgement was that the Kingdom was taken from one generation of Israel and given to another, so that it was postponed. Moreover in place of 7 years of grace under Christ, Israel will have to suffer 7 years of Tribulation under antichrist (v27), which was prefigured by the 7 years of initial judgement (AD 66-73) that happened to that same

generation (v26).   The prophecy clearly links these two judgements together as a dual outworking of the rejection of the Messiah in v26. In the Olivet Discourse Jesus interprets Daniel's prophecy giving more detail about these two judgements that come as a result of their rejection of Him as Messiah (Luke 21, Matthew 24).

The mercy is that God is giving Israel a second chance, and by the end of the 2nd run of Daniel's 70th Week Israel will repent and Jesus will return to save her and destroy the antichrist on the final day of this 70th Week. As He fulfilled the first set of three Messianic accomplishents at the close of the 70th Week in His First Coming, so He will fulfil the second set of three Messianic accomplishents at the close of the 70th Week in His Second Coming.   Therefore Israel's rejection of Christ resulted in a delay, but not a denial of her final Salvation and Kingdom.

Thus v24 will be perfectly fulfilled at the end of the 70th Week and the detailed way this is accomplished is developed in v25-27. The prophecy describes Christ's Coming, His Death, and His rejection by Israel resulting in judgement upon her instead of her receiving the promised Kingdom (v25,26). Then it describes the ultimate fulfilment of the prophecy at the close of a yet future (repeated) 70th Week (v27), so that it will ultimately be fulfilled with Israel's Salvation and Kingdom at the close of 70 Weeks, despite her initial unbelief.

Interpretations of the 70 Weeks tend to stumble over the paradox between v24 where everything is fulfilled on time (after 70 Weeks) by the Messiah, and v26,27 where the Time of Messiah comes and goes and instead of the Kingdom being established Israel comes under judgement and the Kingdom is delayed until a future 70th Week of Tribulation has run. We have now resolved this paradox in the only possible way: The 70th Week is cancelled and repeated again after the Church Age. Whatever was not fulfilled after the first run will be fulfilled after the second run.   If Daniel 9:24 stood alone it would be a failed prophecy, but combined with v25-27 we see how it is being perfectly fulfilled, for even the delay and replay of the 70 Week due to Israel's unbelief is anticipated in the prophecy.   When v25-27 is allowed to interpret v24, we see that Messiah will fulfil the prophecy in 2 stages, the Salvation stage and the Kingdom stage, the Sufferings and the Glory, and indeed this dual outworking of God's Plan is a general characteristic of Messianic Prophecy.

<u>This interpretation accounts for all the aspects of the prophecy</u>:
*It resolves the paradox of the prophecy showing how the Kingdom is established after 70 weeks without dividing the 70th Week off from the 69 weeks.

*The 70 Weeks are seen to run as a unit. All the Messianic acheivements are linked to the end of the 70th Week (v24) and are by nature Jubilee events happening on a Great Jubilee

*The Complexity of the prophecy is due to the fact that God had predetermined a definite period of time to fulfil His purposes for Israel, but that she rejected the Messiah when He came at the close of that time, and God, who knew all this in advance (as revealed by this prophecy), had prepared His response, which was to discipline Israel and give her a second chance later in such a way, that the prophecy would ultimately be fulfilled in the original predetermined time-period for Israel. Within this prophecy is hidden the Mystery of the Church-Age during which time Israel's clock is stopped.

*Messiah is initially seen in His First Coming as the Prince, not the King (v25).
The time of Messiah is defined as starting after the 69th Week and therefore it occupies the 70th Week. He is said to be cut off (killed) after the 69th Week (v26). Why does it not say 'during the 70th Week'?   Because as far as Israel was concerned that 70th Week would be cancelled (blotted out) and rerun again as the future Tribulation (v27).

*The judgements on Israel (past and future) are explained in terms of Israel's unbelief concerning her Messiah. The Tribulation is the rerun of Daniel's 70th Week. Israel's suffering under the antichrist is the result of her rejection of the Christ. Yet He has not rejected her and will save her from antichrist at the end. Overall in this prophecy, God reveals His Sovereignty by declaring His Purposes for Israel and the very Timing of their fulfillment, as well anticipating and describing every obstacle, and then showing how He will fulfil His purpose anyway and in the time-frame He allotted for Israel in the 1st place

*Since the prophecy defines the Tribulation as the Repetition of the original 70th Week (the Time of Messiah), we can account for the timing of the Tribulation. Not only does it explain why it must be 7 years, but why it must be divided into two halves of 3.5 years

(see v27, and other references in Daniel and Revelation to 1260 days, 42 months, etc).

In the 7 years of Grace, the first half of 3.5 years (April AD 26 -October 29) was the preparatory ministry of John the Baptist in the spirit and place of Elijah. In the rerun Israel again have a preparatory ministry, this time of Elijah himself (as one of the 2 witnesses), possibly countered by the false-prophet. It is impossible to understand the scriptures relating John and Elijah if the cancellation and rerun of the 70th Week is not understood. God promised to send Elijah to Israel just before Messiah set up his Kingdom, but knowing Israel would reject it and that it would not be established at the First Coming, He held Elijah back, and sent John in Elijah's place to fulfil His ministry. Instead Moses and Elijah were present on earth to witness the key events of His First Coming (they appeared on the Mount of Transfiguration and afterwards also as 2 men in white). This qualifies them to be the 2 witnesses of Revelation 11 for they will be able to give eyewitness testimony to Israel concerning Christ's First Coming. Therefore Elijah will come to Israel just before the 2nd Coming to fulfil His prophesied ministry to Israel. In the rerun of the 70th Week, he must fulfil a parallel ministry to John's ministry in the original 70th week, calling people to faith in Christ. In particular his ministry must run for the first half of the Week (3.5 years) and that's exactly what we read in Revelation 11

In the 7 years of Grace, the events of the 70th Week come to their climax in second half of 3.5 years (October 29 - April 33) which was the ministry of Jesus Christ himself. This explains why His Ministry was 3.5 years. Likewise in the 7 years of the Tribulation, the events of the re-run 70th Week come to their climax in the second half of the Week, but instead of the 3.5 years of grace under Christ, they must suffer 3.5 years of Great Tribulation under the antichrist (because they rejected Christ). This is why Daniel 9:27 clearly divides the final 70th Week into two halves, with the second half much worse for Israel than the first half, with it being dominated by the antichrist. Moreover in Daniel 9:27 the first half is characterised by the Jews having their Temple, where the prophetic ministry of Moses and Elijah is based for 3.5 years (Revelation 11). So in both runs of the 70th Week, as far as Israel is concerned, the first half is dominated by the prophetic Elijah ministry, and the second half is dominated by the anointed one (either the Christ, anointed by God as the fulfilment of His purposes, or the anti-christ, anointed by satan as the fulfilment of his purposes).

Both 70 Weeks close with a climactic Messianic manifestation on the final day of the 490 years (the Great and Manifest Day of the Lord). The first 70th Week closed with the Resurrection of Christ from the dead. The second 70th Week will close with the Second Coming of Christ in power and glory to save Israel, destroy the antichrist, and establish His Kingdom on earth.

Thus we see a perfect parallelism between the initial Time (7 years) of Messiah and the 7 year Tribulation. This confirms that they are connected in both being the 70th Week of Daniel, and that one is a rerun of the other.

Appendix: One decisive argument against the interpretation of Anderson/Hoehner is that it requires the 70 Weeks to start too early in the year. It is agreed that the start point is Nisan, the first month of the Jewish year, but the issue is when can the New Year begin? This Appendix provides extra evidence that both Anderson and Hoehner require the Nisan in their starting years of 445/444 BC to start too early in the year. Once it is realised Nisan had to start a month later than they say, their whole calculation is invalidated.

*The Biblical Requirement. Beyond dispute is **the Biblical requirement that Passover must be in the Spring** (after the Spring Equinox on March 21st Gregorian). **This by itself requires Nisan to start after the 8th March (Gregorian). This immediately invalides Hoehner's date of February 28th!**

This requirement is confirmed by the Jewish First Century practice as recorded by Philo and Josephus which Christ endorsed by His keeping of the Feasts. It could also be argued that the Bible also requires tabernacles in the 7th month to be in its season after the Autumnal equinox. If this is true then Nisan must start actually after 16th March (Gregorian) which also invalidates Anderson's date of 9th March (Gregorian).

*Jewish practice at that time (500-400 BC) was influenced by the Babylonians who started the year even later, based on the rule that the New Year starts after the Spring Equinox (March 21st Gregorian, which was March 26th Julian at that time). On this basis both Anderson's and Hoehner's dates for Nisan 1 are invalid.

The evidence for this is clear. We have 2 resources that tell us something about the calendar back in the 5th century BC: Jewish scribal papyri from Elephantine, Egypt and cuneiform tablets from Mesopotamia. Both indicate that March 14 is too early in the year to be considered Nisan, the first month of the Jewish year.

At Elephantine, Nisan 1 ranged from March 26 (in 446 and 428 BC) to April 24 (in 465 BC) (Siegfried Horn and Lynn Wood, The Chronology of Ezra 7, p. 157-159).
In Babylonia, Nisan 1 ranged from March 26 to April 23 for the years 464 BC to 400 BC (Richard Parker and Waldo Dubberstein, Babylonian Chronology, p. 32, 33).

Elephantine Results: S. H. Horn and L. H. Wood, published a paper in 1954 in Journal of Near Eastern Studies. This paper is an analysis of fourteen double-dated Jewish papyri from Elephantine, Egypt, which attempts to ascertain the nature of the Jewish calendar in the fifth century BC. Because the papyri were dated in both the Jewish calendar and the Egyptian calendar, and because those double dates can only coincide in particular years and particular months, it is possible to assign definite dates to these documents to within a day. The Julian dates assigned to these papyri in the article, along with the dates of the preceding Nisan 1, appear in the table on the next page:

The Elephantine papyri give us Julian dates for Nisan 1 ranging from March 26 through April 24. Hoehner's proposed date of March 5 (Julian) for Nisan 1 in 444 BC is therefore as much as three weeks earlier than the earliest Nisan 1 in the Jewish colony at Elephantine, Egypt. We can therefore confidentally conclude, based on the very sources that Hoehner cites, that March 5 in 444 BC was actually the first day of Adar (the 12th month).   This is confirmed by Richard A. Parker and Waldo Dubberstein's Babylonian Chronology 626 B.C-A.D. 75 (2nd ed.; Providence, 1956, p. 32) where we find that March 4/5th marked the first day of Adar, while Nisan 1 fell on April 3rd (Julian). In other words, according to the very source cited by Hoehner to prove that Nisan began in March 444 BC (on the Julian calendar), Nisan did not begin until April.

The same arguments apply to Anderson's dates for Nisan 1 in 445 BC. The evidence we have from both the Jewish and Babylonian records is that Nisan did not start until a month later. It would have begun after the new moon of April, not after the new moon of March, making April 13 (Julian) the true Nisan 1, not March 14 (Julian), as Anderson has it.

Thus in 445 and 444 BC, Nisan would have begun after the new moon of April, not after the new moon of March as Anderson & Hoehner need to make their calculation work.

Jewish Date of Papyrus	Julian Date of Papyrus	Preceding Nisan 1
Elul 18	Sept. 12, 471 BC	Apr. 1, 471 BC
Kisl. 18	Jan. 2, 464 BC	Apr. 24, 465 BC
Siv. 20	July 7, 451 BC	Apr. 20, 451 BC
Tam. 18	July 13, 449 BC	Mar. 29, 449 BC
Kisl. 2	Nov. 19, 446 BC	Mar. 26, 446 BC
Ab 14	Aug. 27, 440 BC	Apr. 18, 440 BC
Elul 7	Sept. 15, 437 BC	Apr. 14, 437 BC
Tish. 25	Oct. 30, 434 BC	Apr. 12, 434 BC
Siv. 20	June 12, 427 BC	Mar. 26, 427 BC
Tam. 8	July 11, 420 BC	Apr. 7, 420 BC
Kisl. 3	Dec. 16, 416 BC	Apr. 23, 416 BC
Sheb. 24	Feb. 11, 410 BC	Mar. 28, 411 BC
Mar. 24	Nov. 26, 404 BC	Apr. 10, 404 BC
Adar 20	Mar. 9, 402 BC	Mar. 30, 403 BC

MATTHEW 24   MARK 13   LUKE 21

THE SETTING:
Jesus predicts the destruction of
the Temple (fulfilled AD 70)

MATTHEW 24	MARK 13	LUKE 21
1 Then Jesus went out and departed from the temple, and His disciples came to him to show Him the buildings of the temple.	1 Then as He went out of the temple,	5 Then,
		as some spoke of the temple, how it was adorned with beautiful stones and donations,
	one of His disciples said to Him, "Teacher, see what manner of stones and what buildings are here!"	
2 And Jesus said to them,	2 And Jesus answered and said to him, "Do you see these great buildings?	He said,
"Do not look upon all these things. Assuredly, I say to you,		
		6 These things which you see— the days will come when
not *one* stone shall be left here upon another, that shall not be thrown down."	Not *one* stone shall be left upon another, that shall not be thrown down."	not *one* stone shall be left upon another that shall not be thrown down."
3 Now as He sat on the Mount of Olives,	3 Now as He sat on the Mount of Olives opposite the temple,	7 So
the disciples	Peter, James, John, and Andrew	they
came to Him privately, saying,	asked Him privately,	asked Him, saying,

MATTHEW 24　　MARK 13　　LUKE 21

THE THREE QUESTIONS

QUESTION 1
concerns the sign for the destruction of the Temple

MATTHEW 24	MARK 13	LUKE 21
		"Teacher, but
4 "Tell us, when will these things be?	4 "Tell us, when will these things be?	when will these things be?
	And what will be the sign when all these things will be fulfilled?"	And what sign will there be when these things are about to take place?"

QUESTION 2
concerns the signs for the Second Coming of Christ.

"And what *will be* the sign of Your coming?"

QUESTION 3
concerns the signs for the approach of the Tribulation (the end or consummation, 'suntelia', of the age)

"and of the end of the age?"

THE GENERAL CHARACTERISTICS OF THIS AGE (therefore these are not signs of any of these three events)

MATTHEW 24	MARK 13	LUKE 21
4 And Jesus answered and said to them: "Take heed that	5 ¶ And Jesus, answering them, began to say: "Take heed that	8* And He said: "Take heed that
no one deceives you.	no one deceives you.	you not be deceived.
5 For many will come in My name, saying, 'I am the Christ,'	6* "For many will come in My name, saying, 'I am *He*,'	For many will come in My name, saying, 'I am *He*,' and, 'The time has drawn near.'
and will deceive many.	and will deceive many.	Therefore do not go after them.

MATTHEW 24

6 And you will hear of wars and rumors of wars. See that you are not troubled; for all *these things* must come to pass, but the end ('telos') is not yet.

These previous events do not mean we are in the Tribulation.

THE START OF THE TRIBULATION
(Part of the answer to question 2)

7 *For* (then) nation will rise against nation, and kingdom against kingdom.

And there will be

famines,

pestilences, and earthquakes in various places.

8 All these *are* the beginning of sorrows (birth pains).

9 "Then they will deliver you up to Tribulation and kill you, and you will be hated by all nations for My name's sake.
10 "And then many will be offended, will betray one another, and will hate one another.

MARK 13

7 "But when you hear of wars and rumors of wars, do not be troubled; for *such things* must happen, but the end *is* not yet.

8 *For* (then) nation will rise against nation, and kingdom against kingdom.

And there will be earthquakes in various places, and there will be famines and troubles.

These *are* the beginnings of sorrows.

LUKE 21

9 But when you hear of wars and commotions, do not be terrified; for these things must come to pass first, but the end will not come immediately."

10 Then He said to them, "Nation will rise against nation, and kingdom against kingdom.

11 And there will be great earthquakes in various places, and famines

and pestilences;

and there will be fearful sights and great signs from heaven.

MATTHEW 24	MARK 13	LUKE 21
11 "Then many false prophets will rise up and deceive many.		
12 "And because lawlessness will abound, the love of many will grow cold.		
13 "But he who endures to the end (of the Tribulation) shall be saved (by the Return of Christ).		
14 "And this gospel of the kingdom will be preached in all the world as a witness to all the nations, and then the end ('telos', the Return of Christ) will come." (This is the worldwide preaching of the gospel in the Tribulation)		
		FLASHBACK TO THE FIRST CENTURY (instruction to the disciples for their testimony under persecution)
	9 But watch out for yourselves, for	12 But
		before all these things, they will lay their hands on you and persecute you, delivering you up
	they will deliver you up to councils, and you will be beaten in the synagogues.	to the synagogues and prisons.
	You will be brought before rulers and kings for My sake,	You will be brought before kings and rulers for My name's sake. 13 But it will turn out for you as an occasion
	for a testimony to them. 10 And the gospel must first be preached to all the nations. (This is the world-wide preaching of the gospel in the Church-Age).	for testimony.

MATTHEW 24

MARK 13

LUKE 21

Mark 13:

11 "But

when they arrest *you* and deliver you up, do not worry beforehand, or premeditate what you will speak.

But whatever is given you in that hour, speak that; for it is not you who speak, but the Holy Spirit.

12 "Now brother will betray brother to death, and a father *his* child; and children will rise up against parents and cause them to be put to death.

13 "And you will be hated by all for My name's sake.

But he who endures to the end shall be saved.

Luke 21:

14 Therefore settle *it* in your hearts

not to meditate beforehand on what you will answer;

15 for I will give you a mouth and wisdom which all your adversaries will not be able to contradict or resist.

16 You will be betrayed even by parents and brothers, relatives and friends; and they will put *some* of you to death.

17 And you will be hated by all for My name's sake.

18 But not a hair of your head shall be lost.

19 By your patience possess your souls.

ANSWER TO QUESTION 1
- THE DESTRUCTION OF THE TEMPLE.

When?- in the disciples' generation.

The sign? Jerusalem surrounded by armies (fulfilled in AD67)

20 But when you see Jerusalem surrounded by armies, then know that its desolation is near.

MATTHEW 24

MARK 13

LUKE 21

Provision for the believer's protection in the terrible times of Daniel 9:26:

21 Then let those who are in Judea flee to the mountains, let those who are in her midst depart, and let not those who are in the country enter her.

22 For these are the days of vengeance, that all things which are written

may be fulfilled.

23 But woe to those who are pregnant and to those who are nursing babies in those days! For there will be great distress in the land and wrath upon this people.

24 And they will fall by the edge of the sword, and be led away captive into all nations. And Jerusalem will be trampled by Gentiles until the times of the Gentiles are fulfilled.

THE SIGN OF MID -
TRIBULATION (Daniel 9:27)
and the start of the Great-Tribulation. The Sign-antichrist's Abomination of Desolation. (Answering Question 2 - this sign tells us when Christ's

Coming is 3 and a half years away)

15,16 Therefore when you see the 'Abomination of Desolation,' spoken of by Daniel the prophet, standing in the holy place" (whoever reads, let him understand), then let
those who are in Judea flee

to the mountains.

14 "So when you see the 'Abomination of Desolation,' spoken of by Daniel the prophet, standing where it ought not" (let the reader understand), "then let those who are in Judea flee to the

mountains.

179

MATTHEW 24   MARK 13   LUKE 21

This prophecy is the key to the preservation of the believers in Israel at this time.

17 Let him who is on the housetop not go down

to take anything out of his house.
18 And let him who is in the field not go back to get his clothes.
19 But woe to those who are pregnant and to those who are nursing babies in those days!
20 And pray that your flight may not be in winter or on the Sabbath.
21 For then there will be Great Tribulation, such as has not been since the beginning of the world

until this time, no, nor ever shall be.
22 And unless those days were shortened, no flesh would be saved; but for the elect's sake

those days will be

shortened

(The days are shortened by the personal return of the Lord to save believing Israel).

COUNTERFEIT SIGNS of Christ's Return to be rejected. (Question 2)
23 Then if anyone says to you, 'Look, here *is* the Christ!' or 'There!' do not believe *it*.

15 Let him who is on the housetop not go down into the house, nor enter to take anything out of his house.
16 "And let him who is in the field not go back to get his clothes.
17 "But woe to those who are pregnant and to those who are nursing babies in those days!
18 "And pray that your flight may not be in winter.
19 "For *in* those days there will be Tribulation, such as has not been since the beginning of the creation which God created until this time, nor ever shall be.
20 And unless the Lord had shortened those days, no flesh would be saved; but for the elect's sake, whom He chose, He shortened the days.

21 "Then if anyone says to you, 'Look, here *is* the Christ!' or, 'Look, *He is* there!' do not believe it.

MATTHEW 24	MARK 13	LUKE 21
24 For false christs and false prophets will rise and show great signs and wonders to deceive, if possible, even the elect.	22 "For false christs and false prophets will rise and show signs and wonders to deceive, if possible, even the elect. 23 "But take heed;	
25 See, I have told you beforehand. 26 Therefore if they say to you, 'Look, He is in the desert!' do not go out; *or* 'Look, *He is* in the inner rooms!' do not believe *it*.	see, I have told you all things beforehand.	

The True Signs of the Return of Christ.

| 27 For as the lightning comes from the east and flashes to the west, so also will the coming of the Son of Man be. (it will be visible top all, nobody will have to tell you, as in v23-26) | | |
| 28 For wherever the carcass is, there the vultures will be gathered together. (Where and when?-it will when the the armies of the world gather at Armageddon to destroy Israel). | | |

Blackout:

29 Immediately after the Tribulation of those days	24 But in those days, after that Tribulation,	25 And
		there will be signs in the sun,
the sun will be darkened, and the moon will not give its light;	the sun will be darkened, and the moon will not give its light;	in the moon,
the stars will fall from heaven,	25 the stars of heaven will fall,	and in the stars;
		and on the earth distress of nations, with perplexity, the sea and the waves roaring;

MATTHEW 24

MARK 13

LUKE 21

26 "men's hearts failing them from fear and the expectation of those things which are coming on the earth,

and the powers of the heavens will be shaken.

and the powers in the heavens will be shaken.

for the powers of heaven will be shaken.

30 Then the sign of the Son of Man will appear in heaven, and then all the tribes of the earth will mourn,

and they will see the Son of Man coming on the clouds of heaven with power and great glory.

26 Then they will see the Son of Man coming in the clouds with great power and glory.

27 Then they will see the Son of Man coming in a cloud with power and great glory.

Regathering of Israel
31 And He will send His angels with a great sound of a trumpet, and they will gather together His elect from the four winds,

27 And then He will send His angels,

and gather together His elect from the four winds, from the farthest part of earth to the farthest part of heaven.

from one end of heaven to the other.

Answers to Question 3-
the signs of being in the time just before the Tribulation)

28 Now when these things (the world-conditions in the Tribulation that Jesus described in answering question 2) begin to happen, look up and lift up your heads, because your redemption (the rapture) draws near."

APPENDIX: A HARMONY OF THE OLIVET DISCOURSE

MATTHEW 24

MARK 13

LUKE 21

THE FIG-TREE (Israel)

32 Now learn
this parable
from the Fig Tree:

When its branch has already
become tender
and puts forth leaves,

you know
that summer is near.

33 So you also,
when you see
all these things,
know that
it is near-
-at the doors!

34 Assuredly, I say to you,
this generation
(that sees the Fig-Tree arise)
will by no means
pass away
till all these things
take place.

35 Heaven and earth
will pass away,
but My words will
by no means pass away.

The Rapture - the sign that
the Tribulation is about to begin).

36 But of that day and
hour no one knows,
not even
the angels of heaven,

but My Father only.

28 Now learn
this parable
from the Fig Tree:

When its branch has already
become tender,
and puts forth leaves,

you know
that summer is near.

29 So you also,
when you see
these things happening,
know that
it is near-
-at the doors!

30 Assuredly, I say to you,
this generation

will by no means
pass away
till all these things
take place.

31 Heaven and earth
will pass away,
but My words will
by no means pass away.

32 But of that day and
hour no one knows,
not even
the angels in heaven, nor
the Son,
but only the Father.

29 Then He spoke to them
a parable:
"Look at the Fig Tree,
and all the Trees.

30 When they are
already budding,
you see
and know for yourselves
that summer is now near.

31 So you also,
when you see
these things happening,
know that
the kingdom of God
is near.

32 Assuredly, I say to you,
this generation

will by no means
pass away
till all things
take place.

33 Heaven and earth
will pass away,
but My words will
by no means pass away.

183

MATTHEW 24	MARK 13	LUKE 21
37 But as the days of Noah so also will the coming of the Son of Man be. 38 For as in the days before the flood, they were eating and drinking, marrying and giving in marriage, until the day that Noah entered the ark, 39 and did not know until the flood came and took them all away, so also will the coming of the Son of Man be. 40 Then two men will be in the field: one will be taken and the other left. 41 Two women grinding at the mill: one will be taken and the other left.		
	33 "Take heed,	34 But take heed to yourselves,
42 Watch therefore,	watch and pray;	
		lest your hearts be weighed down with carousing, drunkenness, and cares of this life, and that Day come on you unexpectedly.
for you do not know what hour your Lord is coming.	for you do not know when the time is.	
		35 For it will come as a snare on all those who dwell on the face of the whole earth. 36 Watch therefore, and pray always that you may be counted worthy to escape all these things that will come to pass, and to stand before the Son of Man (in the Rapture)."

184

MATTHEW 24   MARK 13   LUKE 21

MARK 13

34 *For the son of man is*
like a man going to a far
country,
who left his house
and gave authority
to his servants,
and to each his work,
and commanded the
doorkeeper to watch.

35 Watch therefore,
for you do not know
when the master of the
house is coming
-in the evening,
at midnight,
at the crowing of the
rooster,
or in the morning--
36 lest, coming suddenly,
he find you sleeping.

37 And what I say to you,
I say to all: Watch!"

MATTHEW 24

The Thief in the Night.
43 But know this,
that if the master of the
house had known what hour
the thief would come,
he would have watched
and not allowed his house to
be broken into.

44 Therefore you also be
ready, for the Son of Man is
coming at an hour you do
not expect.

Printed in Poland
by Amazon Fulfillment
Poland Sp. z o.o., Wrocław

61710410R00110